An A B C of CONTEMPORARY READING

Richard Kostelanetz

San Diego State University Press
1995

FIRST EDITION

ISBN 1-879691-26-4

For reprinting copyrighted material, the author is grateful to the following:

Madeline Gins for a page from her *Word Rain* (1969), copyright © 1969 by Madeline Gins.
Grove Press for excerpts from *Encyclopedia* (1969), copyright © 1969 by Richard Horn.
Dick Higgins for "Structure (For Cary and Linda)," and miscellaneous prose passages. Venantius Fortunatus (from *George Herbert's Pattern Poems: In Their Tradition* (Unpublished Editions, 1977), copyright © 1977 by Richard C. Higgins
W. Bliem Kern for his "Sound Poetry," reprinted from Richard Kostelanetz's *Text-Sound Texts* (Wm. Morrow, 1980).
Richard Kostelanetz for his visual poems and photographic reproductions of his video and hologram poems, copyright © 1995 by Richard Kostelanetz.
Frank Kuenstler for a page from *Lens* (1964) by permission of the author. Copyright © 1964 by Frank Kuenstler.
Robert Lax for his poem (Journeyman Press, 1975). Copyright © 1975 by Journeyman Press.
Edward Mendelsohn for the Estate of W. H. Auden, for permission to reprint the untitled chart initially published in Richard Kostelanetz's *Essaying Essays* (OOLP, 1975). Copyright © 1975 by Estate of W. H. Auden.
Dr. Hattula Moholy-Nagy for the *Finnegans Wake* chart and miscellaneous prose passages from her father's *Vision in Motion* (Paul Theobald, 1947). Copyright © 1947 by L. Moholy-Nagy; reviewed 1975 by H. Moholy-Nagy.
New Directions for miscellaneous prose passages from *An ABC of Reading* (1934). Copyright © 1936 by Ezra Pound.
Pantheon Books, New York, NY for a page from Gregory Rabassa's translation of Julio Cortazar's *Hopscotch* (1966).
Gerald J. Janecek for his critical prose and translations.
Every effort has been made to locate copyrighted material. Should any omissions or errors have occurred, please direct corrections to the author at P. O. Box 444, Prince St., New York, NY 10012-0008.

ii

We cannot fully participate in modern consciousness unless we can learn to appreciate the significant art of our own day. Just because people have not learned in their youth the habit of enjoyment, they tend to approach contemporary art with closed minds. They submit it to intellectual analysis when it demands intuitive sympathy.
—Herbert Read, "The Place of Art in a University" (1931)

If a revolution fails to produce a new society by self-activity and self-mobilization of revolutionaries, if it does not involve the forging of a self in the revolutionary process, the revolution will once again circumvent those whose lives are to be lived every day and leave daily life unaffected. Out of the revolution must emerge a self that once again takes full possession of the self.
—Murray Bookchin, "Post-Scarcity Anarchy" (1969)

Perhaps the present interest in futurology portends the substitution of the future for the past in the center of our historical consciousness, or our perception of our place in time.
—Herman Kahn and B. Bruce-Briggs, *Things To Come* (1972)

There is no substitute for critical tradition: a continuum of understanding, early commenced. . . . Precisely because William Blake's contemporaries did not know what to make of him, we do not know either, though critic after critic appeases our sense of obligation to his genius by reinventing him. . . . In the 1920s, on the other hand, *something* was immediately made of *Ulysses* and *The Waste Land*, and our comfort with both works after fifty years, including our ease in allowing for their age, seems derivable from the fact that they have never been ignored.
—Hugh Kenner, *The Pound Era* (1971)

[Three rules:] Fiction about history almost never becomes part of the history of fiction. The literature that finally matters in any culture is almost never principally *about* that culture. Whatever else it is about, great literature is almost always also about itself.
—John Barth, *The Friday Book* (1984)

These poems and the whole theory of trans-sense language made a great impression and in their time even caused an immediate literary scandal. The public, which feels obliged to see that art is not damaged by artists, greeted these poems with curses, while the critics, who examined them in the light of science and democracy, rejected them, grieving at the abyss, the *nihil,* to which Russian literature had come. There was also much talk of charlatanism. The furor is over, the "extras" have gone home, the critics have written their feuilletons, and the time has come to try to understand this phenomenon.
Viktor Shklovsky, "On Poetry and Trans-Sense Language" (1916)

CONTENTS

Aphorisms are essentially an aristocratic genre of writing. The aphorist does not argue or explain, he asserts; and implicit in his assertion is a conviction that he is wiser and more intelligent than his readers. For this reason the aphorist who adopts a folksy style with "democratic" diction and grammar is a cowardly and insufferable hypocrite.
—W. H. Auden and Louis Kronenberger, *The Viking Book of Aphorisms* (1966)

While it grows and matures, the new must speak for itself, must remain *self-explanatory*—but the layman is justified by asking for an explanation of the new art now, and it is logical for the artist, *after* creating the new art, to try to become *conscious* of it.
—Piet Mondrian, "The Rationality of Neoplasticism" (1917-18)

The very act of reading a book, starting at the top of the first page and moving from left to right, top to bottom, page after page to the end in a consecutive prearranged manner has become *restrictive and boring.* Indeed, any intelligent reader should feel frustrated and restricted within that preordained system of reading.
—Raymond Federman, "Surfiction: A Position" (1976)

PREFACE

Ezra Pound's purpose in his *ABC of Reading* (1934) was predisposing people to comprehend modernist poetry. As a longer, more resonant sequel to his earlier essay on "How To Read" (1928), this book could have been called an "ABC of Understanding." Pound wanted, with all the intelligence and passion he could command, to sensitize his readers to the new literature he loved and incidentally made. On behalf of his goal, his book recommends, explains, badgers, makes incisive discriminations, and raises critical issues, in addition to offering guidelines, identifying precursors, and reprinting choice examples of the new poetry. Desiring succinct communication, favoring conclusions over patiently developed arguments, Pound made the sentence, not the paragraph, the essential unit of his polemical criticism.

In preparing a comparable essay, similar in style and substance, several decades later, I find that specific recommendations and explanations appear in critical surveys and anthologies published under my name. The badgering I would prefer to avoid.

As in Pound's day, there are pernicious establishments that must be overcome, chiefly because their strictures lamentably narrow the minds of many literate readers. Whereas Pound

An aphoristic tone hangs about this book (*we, one, always*). Now the maxim is compromised in an essentialist notion of human nature, it is linked to classical ideology: it is the most arrogant (often the stupidest) of the forms of language. Why then not reject it? The reason is, as always, emotive: I write maxims (or I sketch their movement) *in order to reassure myself*: when some disturbance arises, I attenuate it by confiding myself to a fixity which exceeds my powers: "*Actually, it's always like that*": and the maxim is born. The maxim is a sort of *sentence-name*, and to name is to pacify. Moreover, this too is a maxim: it attenuates my fear of seeking extravagance by writing maxims.
—Roland Barthes, *Roland Barthes* (1975)

I would like to believe that quotations in this work act less as escutcheon than mosaic of a collective dream. Alternatively— since from time there is no escape—they may constitute a kind of music, gnostic yet full of noise, aspiring Babel and wise babble, the sound of our being here. Distinct from my language, in sound if not sense dissonant, these intertexts offer a context for my text, can become themselves the text and my words quotations.
—Ihab Hassan, *The Right Promethean Fire* (1979)

A book, like a keyboard, is a mechanical device for bringing an entire artistic structure under the interpretative control of a single person. But just as it is possible to distinguish piano music from the piano score of an opera or symphony, so we may distinguish genuine "book literature" from books containing the reduced textual scores of recited or acted pieces.
—Northrop Frye, *Anatomy of Criticism* (1957)

In the matter of education, if the young are not to profit by our sweats, if they are not to pluck the fruits of our experience in the form of better curricula, it might be well to give it up

made a concerted effort to pulverize artistic deadwood in his time, I prefer to think that the current semblances are disintegrating on their own.

By developing themes through a succession of *pensées*, this essay offers some general principles that will, I hope, stimulate perception and instill more percipient attitudes. At best, some of these guidelines will stick in one's head, for among my purposes are saving the reader's time, cordially ushering him or her into a new world of literary experience, ideally accelerating everyone's acceptance and understanding of radically new art.

This is set in a larger typeface than most of my other books because it is meant to be read more slowly.

The principal reason for writing an "ABC" of *Contemporary* reading is that vanguard literature today is considerably different from what Pound had in mind. Thus, criticism of imaginative writing in our time must start again from the ABCs.

One presupposition that ought to be acknowledged at the beginning is that literary art exists in a universe of other arts; thus, post-1960 avant-garde painting and music are relevant to post-1960 vanguard writing (and vice versa). On no fundamental esthetic level, other than emphasizing language, should literature be

altogether. At any rate the critic not aiming at a better curriculum for the serious study of literature is a critic half-baked, swinging in a vacuum.
—Ezra Pound, "Prefatio Aut CimiciumTumulus" (1933)

The following sets out to define an aesthetic drawn from a particular kind of theatrical performance which has been worked out in practice over the past few decades. In the theoretical statements, excursions, technical indications occasionally published in the form of notes to the writer's plays, aesthetics have only been touched on casually and with comparative lack of interest.
—Bertolt Brecht, "A Short Organum of the Theatre" (1948)

All the arts stem from the same and unique root. Consequently, all the arts are identical.
—W. Kandinsky, "The Value of Concrete Work" (1938)

One perception must immediately and directly lead to further perception.
—Charles Olson, "Projective Verse" (1950)

It is written as part of my feeling that an artist must not only create his work but also, if that work presents any difficulties, create a conceptual environment or paradigm in which its difficulties can be surmounted.
—Dick Higgins, "Postscript to Postface. . . ." (1977)

Art in many respects resembles religion. Its development consists not of new discoveries that obliterate old truths and stamp them as false (as is apparently the case in science). Its

considered different from either painting or music.

Another presupposition is that this book describes a real world. It is not about ghosts in some ideological machine but about history (the field in which I received my degrees) and thus favors statements more empirical than speculative or, in the current nomenclature, "interesting." This is criticism meant to be not only insightful but true.

For support in writing this essay I am indebted to countless colleagues who have commented upon it, to editors who have published parts in their journals and books (the earlier versions becoming my equivalent of Pound's "How to Read"), to the Pulitzer Committee that in 1965, in giving me a fellowship that encouaged me to examine the nonliterary arts, laid the groundwork for the perceptions developed here, and to Douglas Turnbaugh of the Ludwig Vogelstein Foundation that in 1980 gave me a grant to revise an earlier draft. One section kept from that draft, "Scientific Revolutions," broaches a theme that, though it has since been vulgarized to death, perhaps survives here. I am also grateful to Charles Doria, Bob Grumman, John Rocco, and Lauren Kozol for critical readings, and to Harry Polkinhorn for publishing.

Richard Kostelanetz   New York, New York

development consists in moments of sudden illumination, resembling a flash of lightning, or explosions that burst in the sky like fireworks, scattering a whole "bouquet" of different-colored stars around them. This illumination reveals with blinding clarity new perspectives, new truths that are in essence nothing other than the organic wisdom, which is not cancelled out by the latter, but remains living and productive as truth and wisdom.
—W. Kandinsky, "Reminiscences/Three Pictures" (1913)

But if artists don't speak and they depend on their lawyers to speak for them, it makes it impossible for anybody else to move into the conversation.
—Barnett Newman, in a symposium (1966)

AVANT-GARDE

The term *avant-garde* refers to those out front, forging a path that others will take. Initially coined to characterize the shock troops of an army, the epithet passed over into art. Used precisely, *avant-garde* should refer, first, to rare work that satisfies three discriminatory criteria: it transcends current conventions in crucial respects, establishing discernible distance between itself and the mass of current practices; it will necessarily take considerable time to find its maximum audience; and it will probably inspire future, comparably advanced endeavors. Only a small minority can ever be avant-garde; for once the majority has caught up to something new, what is genuinely avant-garde, by definition, will be someplace else. The term has the same meaning in English as in French, and thus need not be italicized. It must be a modern concept because the 14th edition (1929) of the *Encyclopedia Britannica* lacks an entry on it. Problems notwithstanding, avant-garde remains a critically useful category.

As a temporal term, avant-garde characterizes art that is "ahead of its time"—that is beginning something—while "decadent" art, by contrast, stands at the end of a prosperous development. "Academic" refers to art that is conceived according to rules that are learned in a

But the new does exist, even apart from any consideration of progress. It is implied in *surprise*. So is the new spirit. Surprise is the most living, the newest element of the new spirit—its mainspring. It is by the element of surprise, by the important place it assigns to surprise, that the new spirit is distinguished from all earlier artistic and literary movements.
—Guillaume Apollinaire, "The New Spirit and the Poets" (1917)

Some artists may accept the limits of art as defined, as known, as given; others may attempt to alter, expand, or escape from the stylistic aesthetic rules passed onto them by the culture. This impulse to redefine, to contradict, to continue the sensed directionality of art as far as they are able, is independent of success. The fact that an artist does not actually succeed in adding anything of importance to the historical development of art does not, in this sense, make the term *avant-garde* inapplicable. It is his intent or desire that is enough to separate him from those who do not share his goals and beliefs.
—Michael Kirby, "The Aesthetics of the Avant-Garde" (1969)

Like so much else in history, the death of the avant-garde never took place; nonetheless, this nonevent really occurred and continues to cast a shadow over its heirs. It occurred because it must have occurred, because a certain logic demanded it. The fact that any current practice might seem to contradict it has not prevented it from reproducing itself in discourse and art.
—Paul Mann, *The Theory Death of the Avant-Garde* (1991)

The term avant-garde can be profitably used to distinguish writers and artists who believe not only that the world they inhabit is essentially modern and that they need to find an aesthetic language to express this newness, but also that they are in some manner in advance of a future state and society which their innovative works will help bring into existence.
—Charles Russell, *Poets, Prophets, and Revolutionaries* (1985)

classroom; it is temporally post-decadent. Whereas decadent art is created in expectation of an immediate sale, academic artists expect approval from their social superiors, whether they be teachers or higher-ranking colleagues. Both academic art and decadent art are essentially opportunistic, created to realize immediate success, even at the cost of surely disappearing from that corpus of art that survives, as the strongest art does, initially by being remembered. By contrast, one fact shared by both decadent art and academic art is that they realize their maximal audience upon initial publication. (Any "literary theory" that fails to deal with avant-garde writing is *ipso facto* academic as well as retrograde.)

Avant-garde art has been defined as "whatever artists can get away with." This is true, however, only in time and in context—only if the invention contributes to an ongoing perceptible tendency or challenges radically an acknowledged professional issue. As avant-garde art is not made in a vacuum, so it is not offered only to the wind. The exact same brand-new creation that might seem innovative at one time or one place can, even if redone precisely, seem irrelevant, if not decadent, at another. The vanguard is the front of the train; the derriere-garde, the caboose. Most artists ride cars in the middle. "Eccentric art" is a reasonable term for work

"Avant-Garde" is merely a convenient metaphor drawn (in the mid-nineteenth century) from the military, in which an avant-garde moves in advance of the main body of troops. "Avant-garde" is relative, not absolute. A conservative poet can be at least morally avant-garde by moving in the direction of ever-greater integrity and purity, or vividness of metaphor and excellence of line. Others seek to follow, even when they cannot; and thus the avant-garde metaphor retains its relevance.
—Dick Higgins, "Intermedia" (1984)

The avant-garde was something constituted from moment to moment by artists—a relative few in each moment—going toward what seemed the improbable. It was only after the avant-garde, as we now recognize it, had been under way for some fifty years that the notion of it seemed to begin to correspond to a fixed entity with stable attributes.
—Clement Greenberg, "Counter-Avant-Garde" (1971)

For a certain moment of history, a picture or a statue speaks a language it will never speak again: the language of its birth.
—André Malraux, *The Imaginary Museum* (1953)

In the case of Duchamp, the antagonism he arouses is an element of his role, and even, if one wishes, of his greatness and profundity.
—Harold Rosenberg, *Art on the Edge* (1975)

Now art should never try to be popular. The public should try to make itself artistic.
—Oscar Wilde, *The Soul of Man under Socialism* (1891)

that is inconsequentially different (and thus *not* avant-garde).

One secondary characteristic of avant-garde art is that, in the course of entering new terrain, it violates entrenched rules—it seems to descend from "false premises" or "heretical assumptions"; it makes current "esthetics" seem irrelevant. For instance, Susanne Langer's theory of symbolism, so prominent in the 1940s and even the 1950s, is hardly applicable to the new art of the subsequent decades. It offers little intelligence toward understanding, say, the music of John Cage or Milton Babbitt, the choreography of Merce Cunningham, the poetry of John Ashbery, where what you see or hear is generally most, if not all, of what there is. This sense of irrelevance is less a criticism of Langer's theories, which seemed so persuasively revelatory in their times, than a measure of drastic difference.

One reason why avant-garde works should be initially hard to comprehend is not that they are intrinsically inscrutible or hermetic but that they defy, and challenge as they defy, the perceptual biases of artistically educated people. They forbid easy access or easy acceptance, as an audience perceives them as inexplicably different, if not forbiddingly revolutionary. In order to begin to comprehend avant-garde art, people must work and think in unfamiliar ways. Nonetheless, if people learn to accept innovative

All arts tend to decline into the stereotype; and at all times the mediocre tend to try, semi-consciously or unconsciously, to obscure the fact that the day's fashion is not the immutable.
—Ezra Pound, "*Vers Libre* and Arnold Dolmetsch" (1917)

Beginnings: Nothing less is intended than a revolution in thought with writing as the fulcrum, by means of which—and the accidental place, any place, therefore America—one like another, therefore where we happen to be, our locality, as base.
—William Carlos Williams, *The Embodiment of Knowledge* (1974)

The new novel is merely pursuing a constant evolution of the genre. . . . The construction of our books is, moreover, disconcerting only if one insists on looking in them for the trace of elements which have actually disappeared in the last twenty, thirty or forty years from all living novels or have at least disintegrated: characters, chronology, sociological studies, etc. . . . If the reader sometimes has difficulty in getting his bearings in the modern novel, it is the same way that he sometimes loses them in the very world where he lives, when everything in the old structures and the old norms around him is giving way.
—Alain Robbe-Grillet, "New Novel, New Man" (1961)

The avant-garde consists of those who feel sufficiently at ease with the past not to have to compete with it or duplicate it.
—Dick Higgins, "Does Avant-Garde Mean Anything?" (1970)

Art may not change the world, but it is made by those who would like to change it.
—Seldon Rodman, *Tongues of Fallen Angels* (1974)

work, it will stretch their perceptual capabilities, affording them kinds of sensory experience previously unknown. Edgard Varèse's revolutionary *Ionisation* (1931), for instance, taught a generation of listeners about possible coherence and beauty in what they had previously perceived as noise, just as cubism taught viewers of painting how to reconfigure space and then time.

It follows that avant-garde art usually offends people, especially serious artists, before it persuades; and it offends them not in terms of content, but in terms of Art. They assert that Varèse's noise (or Cage's, or John Zorn's) is unacceptable as music. That explains why avant-garde art strikes most of us as esthetically "wrong" before a few of us acknowledge it as possibly "right"; it "fails" before we recognize that it *works*. (Art that offends by its content offends only as journalism or gossip, rather than as Art, and is thus as likely to disappear as quickly as other journalism or gossip.)

Those most antagonized by the avant-garde are not the general populace, which does not care, but the guardians of culture, who do, whether they be cultural bureaucrats, established artists or their epigones, because *they* feel, as they sometimes admit, "threatened."

Disreputably unforgettable or commendably forgotten—given the chance, the avant-grade artist would prefer that his creation be the

It takes approximately twenty years to make an artistic curiosity out of a modernistic monstrosity; and another twenty to elevate it to a masterpiece.
—Nicholas Slonimsky, *Lexicon of Musical Invective* (1953)

A revolution of the content—socialism—anarchism—is unthinkable without a revolution of form—Futurism.
—Vladimir Mayakovsky, *Newspaper of Futurists* (1918)

Until quite recently, one could read a book or contemplate a painting without knowing the exact period during which it was brought into being. Many such works were held up as "timeless" models beyond all chronological servitude. Today, however, all undated reality seems vague and invalid, having the insubstantial forms of a ghost.
—Julián Marías, *Generations: A Historical Method* (1970)

For a very long time everybody refuses and then almost without a pause almost everybody accepts. In the history of the refused in the arts and literature the rapidity of the change is always startling. When the acceptance comes, by that acceptance the thing created becomes a classic. It is a natural phenomena, a rather extraordinary natural phenomena that a thing accepted becomes a classic. And what is the characteristic quality of a classic. The characteristic quality of a classic is that it is beautiful. . . . Of course it is beautiful but first all beauty in it is denied and then all the beauty of it is accepted. If every one were not so indolent they would realize that beauty is beauty even when it is irritating and stimulating not only when it is accepted and classic.
—Gertrude Stein, "Composition as Explanation" (1926)

former. That is one explanation for why those new works that veterans dismiss while new artists debate are usually avant-garde.

Though vanguard activity may dominate discussion among sophisticated professionals, it never dominates the general making of art. Most work created in any time, in every art, honors long-passed models. Even today, in the United States, most of the fiction written and published and reviewed has, in form, scarcely progressed beyond early twentieth century standards; most poetry today is similarly decadent.

The "past" that the avant-garde aims to surpass is not the tradition of art but the currently decadent fashions; for in Harold Rosenberg's words, "Avant-garde art is haunted by fashion." Because avant-gardes in art are customarily portrayed as succeeding each other, the art world is equated with the world of fashion, in which styles also succeed each other. However, in both origins and function, the two are quite different. *Fashion* relates to the sociology of remunerative taste; *avant-garde,* to the history of art. Fashion by definition is what rapidly goes out of fashion. In practice, avant-garde activity has a dialectical relationship with fashion, for the emerging lucrative fashions can usually be characterized as a synthesis of advanced art, whose purposes are antithetical to those of fashion, with more familiar stuff. When fashion appears to echo

The situation of [Arnold] Schoenberg is typical—he was never in fashion and now he's become old-fashioned.
—Milton Babbitt, *Words about Music* (1987)

The art of the critic in a nutshell: to coin slogans without betraying ideas. The slogans of an inadequate criticism peddle ideas to fashion.
—Walter Benjamin, *One-Way Street* (1925-26)

Art is not predictable. To put it the other way around, what can be predicted is not art. Art which does not surprise, does not enlarge, does not extend our knowledge, our consciousness, our *something*, is not—by twentieth-century standards at least—worth the bother. So we can't talk about its future profitably. We can only talk round it and across it, or we can talk about it from the other side.
—Reyner Banham, "The Future of Art from the Other Side" (1967)

The stammering newborn work will always be regarded as a monster, even by those who find experiment fascinating. There will always be some curiosity, of course, some gestures of interest, and always some provision for the future. And some praise; though what is sincere will always be addressed to the vestiges of the familiar, to all those bonds from which the new work has not yet broken free and which desperately seek to imprison it in the past. . . . Hence it will be the specialists in the novel (novelists or critics, or overassiduous readers) who have the hardest time dragging themselves out of its rut.
—Alain Robbe-Grillet, "A Future for the Novel" (1956)

The Talented Tenth was to be the *avant-garde*, the first wave of Negroes who were to lower the color barriers.
—Elliott M. Rudwick, *W. E. B. DuBois* (1968)

advanced art, a closer look reveals the governing model to be art actually of a period recently past.

One difference between literature and visual art is that the merchandisers of the latter can successfully peddle the work of certain figures who were once genuinely avant-garde, although such produce is itself rarely avant-garde. For example, the purveyors of Salvador Dali can profit at levels unavailable to the purveyors of Gertrude Stein; the former artist can be commercially fashionable to a degree that the latter cannot.

Though fashion imitates the tone of innovation and exploits the myth of its value, the aim of fashion is standardization; the goal of fashion's creators is, simply, a formula that can be successfully mass-merchandised. That accounts for Jean Cocteau's formulation of fashion as what goes out of fashion, as any overworked formula eventually must. The avant-garde artist, by contrast, is interested in discovery and going beyond not only current fashions but also oneself (and, by extension, his or her own previous art).

When avant-garde inventions become fashionable—as, say, collage in visual art and associational syntax in poetry already have—then they begin to seem decadent, so that everyone aspiring to create genuine vanguard art feels in his or her gut that this new fashion has become a milestone that one is obliged to transcend.

The best artists of the twentieth century are great failures.
They can't do what they set out to do.
—Harold Rosenberg, "On Violence in Art and Other Matters" (1969)

The avant-garde, like any culture, can only flower in a climate where political liberty triumphs, even if it often assumes a hostile pose toward democratic and liberal society. Avant-garde art is by its nature incapable of surviving not only the persecution, but even the protection or the official patronage of a totalitarian state and a collective society. . . . The only omnipresent or recurring political ideology within the avant-garde is the least political or the most antipolitical of all: libertarianism and anarchism.
—Renato Poggioli, *The Theory of the Avant-Garde* (1963)

Art is the most intense mode of individualism that the world has known. . . .The form of government that is most suitable to the artist is no government at all.
—Oscar Wilde, *The Soul of Man under Socialism* (1891)

Art is born of freedom and liberty, and dies of constraint.
—David Smith, "Modern Sculpture and Society" (1940)

If, for the better development of the forces of material production, the revolution must build a socialist regime with centralised control, to develop intellectual creation an anarchist regime of individual liberty should from the first be established.
—André Breton, with Leon Trotsky, "Manifesto for an Independent Revolutionary Art" (1938)

Whenever the current state of an art is generally perceived as decadent or expired, a new avant-garde is destined to arise. Even though anarchists in the 1870s founded a short-lived journal called *Avant-Garde*, the political avant-garde ("left") does not always coincide with the esthetic vanguard (also "left"), the latter regarding the former as culturally insensitive and humanly exploitative, and the former regarding the latter as individualistic and politically inept. Each thinks the other is naive about cultural change; and needless to say perhaps, each is essentially correct.

The term avant-garde can also refer to individuals creating such path-forging art; but even by this criterion, the work itself, rather than the artist's intentions, is the ultimate measure of the epithet's applicability to an individual. Thus, an artist or writer is avant-garde only at certain crucial points in his or her creative career, and only those few works that were innovative at their debut comprise the history of modern avant-garde art. The phrase may also refer to artistic groups, if and only if most of its members are (or were) crucially contributing to authentically exploratory activity.

The term is sometimes equated with cultural antagonism, for it is assumed that the "avant-garde" leads artists in their perennial war against the Philistines. However, this retro-

Anarchism. . . is a natural creed for those who consider themselves aesthetically and socially in the avant-garde and therefore opposed to the existing order. Anarchists, moreover, have been less tempted to set rules for artistic creation than other groups, and more inclined to accept art for what it is as it comes from the artist's workshop.
—Francis M. Naumann & Paul Avrich, "Adolf Wolff," *Drunken Boat* 1 (1991)

Anarchist insubordination to authority, like the perpetual struggle to realize the self, is at best a never ending process. There is no final solution, no ultimate reconciliation between subject and object, no day after the revolution, no Eden that will ever grace all of human society.

Rebellion constitutes the essence of life, each act of insubordination gives rise to an existential individualism and with it the dynamic creativity with which everyone is gifted. As such, rebellion is at the same time a rejection of all that which inhibits and destroys one's creative capacity and the process of discovering what a creative existence might mean.
—Max Blechman, "Toward an Anarchist Aesthetic," *Drunken Boat* 2 (1994)

It is possible, as this process of exhaustion goes on, we might eventually reach the point where there is nothing left, where all literary traditions become played out entirely. I suspect that we are approaching that point right now.

If we have reached the end of literary tradition, it doesn't necessarily allow that there will be no more literature, only that we will no longer have "novels" and "poems" and "dramas" in the old senses of the terms, and that terminology such as "naturalistic" or "surrealist" will no longer seem very adequate. Each work of literature will be a unique *gesture* that transcends all the old categories.
—Richard Morris, "A Dadaist Manifesto" (1982)

grade antagonism is a secondary characteristic, as artists' social position and attitudes descend from the fate of their creative efforts, rather than the reverse. Any artist who sets out just to mock the Philistines is not likely to do anything significant artistically.

Avant-garde has nothing to do with gender, geography, social class, sexual persuasion, age, current affiliations, or outside hobbies; it remains a pure category in an era of distraction and vulgarization.

Certain conservative critics have recently asserted that "the avant-garde no longer exists," because, as they see it, the suburban public laps up all new art. However, it is critically both false and ignorant to use a secondary characteristic in lieu of a primary definition. *Avant-garde* is an art-historical term, not a sociological category. If an art critic in particular fails to use "avant-garde" as primarily an art-historical term, then he or she is exploiting the authority of his or her position to spread needless confusion. The fact that the avant-garde is widely discussed, as well as written about, scarcely makes it fashionable or lucrative—not at all.

The conservative charge is factually wrong as well, as nearly all avant-gardes in art are ignored by the middle-class publics (and their agents in the culture industries), precisely because innovative work is commonly perceived as

All original composition—classical, standard, or advance-guard—occurs at the limits of the artist's knowledge, feeling, and technique. Being a spontaneous act, it risks, supported by what one has already grown up to, something unknown.
—Paul Goodman, "Advance-Guard Writing in America," *Kenyon Review* (1951)

Imagine this scenario: a criminologist calls a press conference to announce that crime is dead, that it died of its very proliferation, that it died precisely because everyone knew it existed, because we are surrounded by images of crime and this spectacle renders criminality a mere hoax. After the press conference he returns to his laboratory to find it vandalized, his research destroyed, his equipment looted; he is not greatly bothered by the destruction of so superfluous a facility as a laboratory for studying what no longer exists and perhaps never did. And when the press turns up at his devastated lab and demands to know whether the existence of people who could lay waste to his life's work proves the absurdity of his ideas, he replies that, on the contrary, his certainty that these events would be reported and discussed only ratifies the truth of his theory. Such a scientist would be a laughing stock . . . yet as we have seen, as we see everywhere in avant-garde discourse, it is very much this sort of travesty that characterizes obituaries of the avant-garde.
—Paul Mann, *The Theory-Death of the Avant-Garde* (1991)

"peculiar," if not "unacceptable," not only by the mass public but also by those middlemen who make a business of selling large quantities. Indeed, the pervasiveness of those perceptions is a patent measure of a work's being art-historically ahead of its time. Those denying the survival of the avant-garde resemble those who deny the persistence of economic poverty, each by its fakery making a wish, rather than describing reality, in addition to implicitly rationalizing retrograde attitudes and perhaps the retention of tenuous privileges.

It is also erroneous to think of current avant-gardes as necessarily extending or elaborating previous avant-gardes. It was misleading, for instance, to classify the painter Jasper Johns as only a descendant of Dada, for implicit in Johns's best art is a conceptual leap that reflects Dada and yet moves well beyond it. Partial resemblances to Dada notwithstanding, Johns's work reflects other esthetic purposes, other interests, and other assumptions. Indeed, the term avant-garde is most appropriate when it is applied to work that is so different in intention and effect that it renders the old classifications insufficient. Indeed, in reverse, if it isn't extreme, it probably isn't avant-garde. Extremism may be often be a vice in politics; in art it is nearly always a virtue.

KARAWANE

jolifanto bambla ô falli bambla
grossiga m'pfa habla horem
égiga goramen
higo bloiko russula huju
hollaka hollala
anlogo bung
blago bung
blago bung
bosso fataka
ü üü ü
schampa wulla wussa ólobo
hej tatta gôrem
eschige zunbada
wulubu ssubudu uluw ssubudu
tumba ba- umf
kusagauma
ba - umf

—Hugo Ball

Because the avant-garde claims to be prophetic, the ultimate judge of current claims can only be a future cultural public. For now, a future-sensitive critic should just try to posit tentative estimates. One reason why the artistic innovations of the future cannot be described today is that whatever will be judged avant-garde transcends, almost by definition, current imagination.

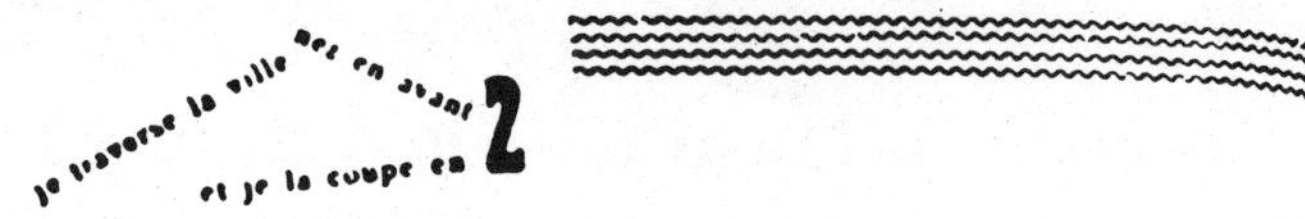

J'étais au bord du Rhin quand tu partis pour le Mexique
Ta voix me parvient malgré l'énorme distance
Gens de mauvaise mine sur le quai à la Vera Cruz

Les voyageurs de *l'Espagne* devant faire
le voyage de Coatzacoalcos pour s'embarquer
je t'envoie cette carte aujourd'hui au lieu

Juan Aldama

Correos
Mexico
4 centavos

YPIRANGA

REPUBLICA MEXICANA
TARJETA POSTAL

11 45
20 5
11
Rue des Batignolles

de profiter du courrier de Vera Cruz qui n'est pas sûr
Tout est calme ici et nous sommes dans l'atten
des événements.

U. S. Postage
2 cents 2

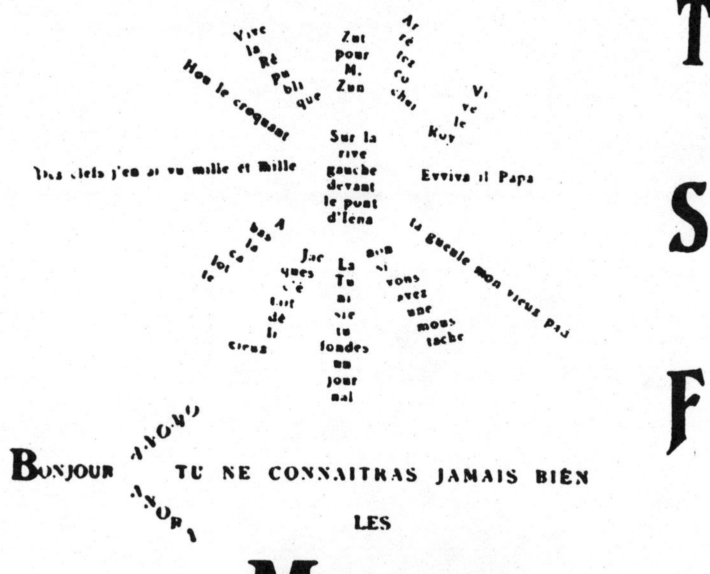

—Guillaume Apollinaire

ORIGINALITY

It is untrue to say that, "There is nothing new under the sun," for always there have been, and always there will be, certain works that are formally so original that, were they presented to a jury of twelve experts, the sages would unanimously agree that, yes, this has not been done before. To the *Oxford English Dictionary*, "innovation" is simply "the alteration of what is established by the introduction of new elements or forms." Few literate people have ever denied the spectacular originality of, say, James Joyce's *Finnegans Wake*; every expert panel would unanimously agree to that.

Nonetheless, even the most innovative art resembles more conservative work in revealing the influence of one or another work of previous art, but what separates the two is the extent of difference. Though Stéphane Mallarmé's *Un Coup de Dés* (1897) reflected certain preoccupations of earlier French poetry, it was also drastically different in certain respects, such as the disjunctiveness of its syntax and its use of the entire space available on the printed page.

Other purposes notwithstanding, every artist ultimately wants to make something that will be remembered—that will stand out from the mass of art that floods the audience interested in it. Distinct originality is one way of insuring that

The scientist does not expect to be acclaimed as a great scientist until he has *discovered* something. He begins by learning what has been discovered already. He goes from that point onwards. He does not bank on being a charming fellow personally. He does not expect his friends to applaud the results of his freshman class work.
—Ezra Pound, "Imagisme" (1913)

In our era, art that ceases to seek the new becomes at once intellectually insignificant, a species of homecraft. The nature of originality is open to debate—in fact, needs desperately to be debated. But no disagreement exists regarding the value of the new art.
—Harold Rosenberg, "Criticism and Its Premises" (1965)

It is hard to imagine a text more fully committed to experimentalism than [Oswald Wiener's *Die Verbesserung von Mitteleuropa, Roman* (*The Improvement of Central Europe, Novel,* 1969)]. Beginning with an index of names and concepts and concluding with a bibliography of some 1,200 entries, this melange of theory and fiction, aphorism, narrative and disquisition, parody and programmatic statement in fact represents a kaleidoscopic but sustained meditation on the regularization of life by the state.
—David E. Wellbury, "On Recent German Writing" (1985)

Well, you know or don't you kennet or haven't I told you every telling has ataling and that's the he and the she of it. Look, look, the dusk is growing! My branches lofty are taking root. And my cold cher's gone ashley. Fieluhr? Filou! What age is at? It saonis late. 'Tis endles now senne eye or erewone last saw Waterhouse's clogh. They took it asunder, I hurd them sigh. When will they reassemble it? O, my back, my back, my bach!

a work will be noticed and thus preserved. The overwhelming bulk of current art makes the audience's perception of genuine originality a more crucial element in artistic experience than it was before.

Much original art initially strikes us as palpably incredible. It is hard for the spectator to believe that individual human beings made such works as *Finnegans Wake,* Simon Rodia's Watts Towers, Charles Ives's Fourth Symphony, Pound's *Cantos*, etc. They exceed our sense of the capabilities of human imaginative realization; they are literally too much. Indeed, this feeling of incredulity must be classified as esthetic, because it surely is not anything else.

Sometimes this incredible originality is entwined with an offensive quality. How can anyone claim that there is Art—that Art exists—in the utter simplicity of minimal sculpture, in the elliptical style of *Naked Lunch*, or in the restricted vocabulary of Dick Higgins' *Structure* (1970), in which three stanzas with 36 separate verbal units contain only four discrete words! Of course, the more familiar we become with such work, and other art like it, the less offensive such originality becomes. Eventually, even the conservative's skepticism disappears.

Pound speaks of literary inventors as "men who found a new process, or whose extant work gives us the first known example of a process."

I'd want to go to Aches-les-Pains. Pingpong! There's the Belle
for Sexaloitez!
—James Joyce, *Finnegans Wake* (1939)

The aim of every authentic artist is not to conform to the history
of art but to release himself from it, in order to replace it with
his own history.
—Harold Rosenberg, *Art on the Edge* (1975)

The Formalist movement had ever since its inception made
common cause with the artistic *avant-garde*. In their early
writings, [Viktor] Shklovskii and [Roman] Jakobson sought to
elevate the Futurist experiments into general laws of poetics.
. . . Clearly, in the Formalist responses to contemporary
literature, the diagnosis mattered more than the prescription,
the will to change was more crucial—and more widely shared—
than the commitment to a particular set of innovations. Whatever the nature or direction of the literary 'upheaval' cham-
pioned at the moment, the emphasis of Formalist criticism was
invariably on the bold and uninhibited search for novelty; its
watchword—'inventiveness' (*izobretatel'stvo*) .
—Victor Erlich, *Russian Formalism* (1955)

Art, if you want a definition, is criminal action. It conforms to
no rules, not even its own.
—John Cage, *A Year from Monday* (1967)

By these criteria, Pound himself was an inventor; so were Faulkner, Beckett, and Gertrude Stein at crucial points in their creative lives. Invention, in technology as in art, is the creation of something decisively unlike anything and everything that went before.

Originality of this kind is, to repeat, indubitably verifiable; indeed, it is almost measurable.

Eccentricity defines personal peculiarity; originality exists outside oneself. On rare occasions, the two coincide. Originality that is not avant-garde is essentially eccentric.

The community of art, by common consent, bestows a kind of patent upon genuine invention. Thus, the artist who uses it without either change or acknowledgment is customarily accused of "plagiarism." If a later artist turns another man's innovation to personal uses, then his or her work is initially characterized as "imitative" or "derivative." Such reminders do not invalidate new work; instead, they give it an art-historical definition.

If we take the regimentation of response to be humanly pernicious, then the interruption of expectation is morally superior. As everyday life is characterized by recurrence and predictability, we turn to art for invention and surprise. One practical function of innovative art is preparing the perceptual faculties for the puzzling forms in

structure (for cary and linda)

pearls, pearls of pearls
      pearls, pearls of garlic
            pearls, pearls of leaves

pearls, garlic of pearls
      pearls, garlic of garlic
            pearls, garlic of leaves

pearls, leaves of pearls
      pearls, leaves of garlic
            pearls, leaves of leaves

garlic, pearls of pearls
      garlic, pearls of garlic
            garlic, pearls of leaves

garlic, garlic of pearls
      garlic, garlic of garlic
            garlic, garlic of leaves

garlic, leaves of pearls
      garlic, leaves of garlic
            garlic, leaves of pearls

leaves, pearls of pearls
      leaves, pearls of garlic
            leaves, pearls of leaves

leaves, garlic of pearls
      leaves, garlic of garlic
            leaves, garlic of leaves

leaves, leaves, of pearls
      leaves, leaves of garlic
            leaves, leaves of leaves.

—Dick Higgins (1970)

the changing scene around us. By contrast, people who are blinded by innovative art (or allow themselves to be) are liable to be similarly befuddled about what is most original in contemporary life. Given the fact of historical change, our perception of art, like our awareness of reality, must continually be updated. On this level, original art can be socially useful without undermining its own integrity.

And it is true to say that a new idea of art has arisen in our times, as it arose when Leonardo's art and Titian's replaced that of the nameless sculptors of the cathedrals.
—André Malraux, *The Imaginary Museum* (1953)

Thought and speech cannot keep up with what an inspired man experiences, therefore the artist is free to express himself not only in ordinary language (concepts), but in a personal language (a creator is individual), a language which has no precise meaning (which is not ossified), which is trans-sensible, *zaumnyi*. Ordinary language restricts, free language allows freer expression (e.g., *Go, osnet, Kayt,* etc.). Words die, the world is always young. The artist has seen the world anew and, like Adam, gives to everything its name. The lily is wonderful, but the word *lily* is ugly, it is worn out and "raped." So I name the lily *euy* and the original purity is restored.

Verse unwittingly gives us a series of vowels and consonants. These series are inviolable. It is better to replace words with something else close not in sense but in sound (lyki-myki-kika).
—A. Kruchonykh, "Declaration of the Word as Such" (1913)

As a practicing critic, I once thought that literature need not be "new" to be good. Criticism of the "new" was merely a specialty of mine; it was only one of several strong critical interests.

I later believed that a work might be "better" if it were new as well as "good"—its innovative quality became a positive increment, so to speak, upon its artistic base.

Then I judged that a work was not consequential unless it were new, because only by realizing significant innovations did it earn a place in the history of art. By this time I was avoiding questions of quality.

By now it is clear to me that simply by being radically innovative, simply by discovering possibilities for literary art, a work is worthwhile, both esthetically and ethically. Simply, if a new work does not particularly resemble anything done before—if it is clearly original—it is good, solely for that reason. Thus, only by incorporating innovation can a work be truly significant; only what is new deserves serious consideration.

Though art may not get "better," what does indeed improve is our critical comprehension of how art is created and perceived. Nothing is so inscrutable that its uniqueness cannot be persuasively defined eventually. As what was once inscrutable is now taught to undergraduates,

Whereas most people readily accept the idea that the history of science demonstrates progress, in art they are unwilling to accept the idea of anything but change. Science, it is claimed, continually outgrows its older ideas, but the validity of great art remains permanent.
—Suzi Gablik, *Progress in Art* (1976)

Only after it occurs does progress become an obvious characteristic of a field.
—Thomas S. Kuhn, *The Structure of Scientific Revolutions* (1962)

It must not be forgotten that we are the first to realize that every art is closely bound up with a significance peculiar to itself: until our times such forms as did not tally with a preconceived significance of art were not linked up with *other* significances, but relegated to the scrap heap.
—André Malraux, *The Imaginary Museum* (1953)

Nothing is good save the new. If a thing has novelty it stands intrinsically beside every other work of artistic excellence. If it have not that, no loveliness or heroic proportion or grand manner will save it.
—William Carlos Williams, *Kora in Hell: Improvisations* (1920)

Newness (not novelty) may be the highest individual value in poetry. Even in the meretricious sense of newness a new poetry has value.
—Wallace Stevens, "Adagia," *Opus Posthumous* (1957)

what does evidently progress is our acceptance of innovation. If our capacities for artistic perception increase measurably, then it is reasonable to conclude that our esthetic experience does indeed expand.

The essence of progress in artistic understanding, for both creator and perceiver, comes from the continual subjection of oneself to the challenges of unfamiliar work.

There is no ultimate plateau to either art or perception. No one except Ad Reinhardt could assuredly accept his contention that he had made "the last painting which anyone can make." The attempt to transcend time seems doomed, because everything done yesterday can be surpassed in one way or another. There is no end, only change and, yes, progress.

The important thing is that we approached art systematically. We spoke about art as such. We refused to view it as a reflection. We located the distinctive features of the genus. We began defining the basic tendencies of form. We understood that, in fact, you can distill from works of literature the homogeneous laws that determine their shape. In short, a science is possible.
—Viktor Shklovsky, *The Third Factory* (1926)

EXPERIMENTAL

Avant-garde writing resembles experimental science in that both incorporate, to quote my *Webster's,* "an action or process undertaken to discover something not yet known." In a broad sense, all imaginative writing could be considered "experimental," as writers are continually making literature that, short of plagiarism, does not already exist.

However, only those forays that courageously court the unknown—that structurally go well beyond established conventions—finally deserve the honorific epithet. Francis Bacon, the father of experimental science, noted in *The New Organon* (1620): "It would be unsound and self-contradictory to expect things which have never been done can be done except by means which have never been tried."

Bertolt Brecht once said: "Only new contents permit new forms." It is more true to say, however, that new forms permit, as well as generate, new contents—only with new media, with new methods, can the poet or the scientist discover new ends. Indeed, new contents are better presented in older forms, precisely because unfamiliar experiences are more easily understood and communicated in familiar formats. That is the basic stylistic wisdom of journalism. Conversely, if a writer wants to

Language as a real thing is not imitation either of sounds or colors or emotions it is an intellectual recreation and there is no possible doubt about it and it is going to go on being as long as humanity is anything. So everyone must stay with the language their language that has come to be spoken and written and which has in it all the history of its intellectual recreation.
—Gertrude Stein, *Lectures in America* (1935)

The political revolutionary does not refuse to cast his revolutionary songs in the modal structure and scale progressions of the culture he is in the process of changing. . . . The one who rebels against the religious and moral system of his time will couch his appeals in the linguistic patterns of his people, use established affect symbols, and employ accepted esthetic standards in heightening the responses of his followers.
—Melville Hershkovits, "On Cultural and Psychological Reality" (1951)

Invention is, then, a continuous social process without clear beginning or end. The development of a new product or process is a series of inventions, each of which responds to the problems of earlier efforts and creates new problems requiring solutions.
—Donald A. Schon, *Technology and Change* (1967)

Indeed, the work of many artists often comes closer to philosophical speculation than most aesthetic writings, which retrace the same ground over and over, sometimes systematically and sometimes historically, but rarely with originality. . . . The major artistic inventions, on the other hand, resemble modern mathematical systems in the freedoms with which their creators discarded certain conventional assumptions and replaced them with others.
—George Kubler, *The Shape of Time* (1962)

experiment with unfamiliar forms, it might be wise for him or her to choose a familiar subject.

In art as well as science, unless you begin differently, you've not begun at all but are merely contributing to established enterprise. Art and science also share the principle that serious work is done initially not for a large audience but for one's peers. It follows that the most consequential experiments are those which are acknowledged by at least some fellow workers; and one practical measure of the value of a current experiment is the willingness of its initial audience to communicate news of it to their own immediate audiences. A second measure is its capacity to inspire further experiment.

At first I planned to echo the familiar sentiment that, "An artistic experiment may be 'successful' on its own terms, but irrelevant to any larger contexts, simply because it fails to generate any further exploration." However, the more closely I considered that sentence, the less tenable it seemed, because I was unable to think of any step-ahead artistic experiment that did not eventually have some sort of perceptible impact upon future art.

Some artistic experiments are, in truth, based upon personal incompetence. When Arnold Schoenberg told his pupil John Cage that he had no talent for harmony, the younger composer disregarded harmony in his own musical experiments.

Every painter of genius . . . does not necessarily want to change the world, nor does he seek to justify God's ways to man; he wants to challenge existing pictures with pictures that do not yet exist.
—André Malraux, *The Imaginary Museum* (1953)

The Kwakiutal artist painting on a hide did not concern himself with the inconsequentials that made up the opulent social rivalries of the Northwest Coast Indian scene, nor did he, in the name of a higher purity, renounce the living world for the meaningless materialism of design. The abstract shape he used, his entire plastic language, was directed by a ritualistic will toward metaphysical understanding . . . the idea-complex that makes contact with mystery—of life, of men, of nature, of the hard black chaos that is death, or the grayer, softer chaos that is tragedy. For it is only the pure idea that has meaning. Everything else has everything else.
—Barnett Newman, *The Ideographic Picture* (1947)

We always kept the so-called experimental writers apart from the rest—on the shelves as well as in the catalogues [of the Gotham Book Mart]. This seemed natural, since they had no respect for the conventional writers, nor did the conventional writers think seriously of them.
—Frances Steloff, "In Touch with Genius" (1975)

I know how difficult it is for many people to "read"—especially when the writing is in abstract form. "The spectator" is often shocked, because it seems to him as if the ground has been torn away from under his feet—he "drifts." Especially today, it is expected that the "normal individual" should stand solidly with both feet on the ground. Unfortunately, he accedes to this demand

When young Gertrude Stein was advised that her writing was often ungrammatical, she made her principal experiment the possibilities of agrammatical English. In our time, experiments with insufficiency are more interesting, more sympathetic, and ultimately more heroic than the exploitation of virtuosity.

One measure of "success" in literary creation is whether the language of a work creates its own world—whether it is stylistically consistent in itself—and one measure of experimental success is whether or not this language has appeared in print before. Ideally, an experimental writer continually reinvents language anew. What makes Gertrude Stein more significant than Thomas Wolfe, say, is that she invented not one alternative style but several.

In both art and science, there is no future in doing what has already been done. Pound: "Willingness to experiment is not enough, but unwillingness to experiment is mere death."

Marcel Duchamp's reputation is based upon the quality not of his craftsmanship but of his inventions.

Pound: "The scientist does not expect to be acclaimed a great scientist until he has discovered something."

Historically, the great experiments in literature, and thus the great discoveries, focused upon technique, rather than reportage.

too often and obviously forgets that the ancient dream of flying
has come true in our time.
—W. Kandinsky, "Assimilation of Art" (1937)

The social function of the arts, therefore, seems to be closely
connected with visualizing the goal of work in human life. So in
terms of significance, the central myth of art must be the vision
of the end of social effort, the innocent world of fulfilled
desires, the free human society.
—Northrop Frye, "The Archetypes of Literature" (1951)

Experimental (that is, lacking a realistic expectation of finan-
cial success). . . .
—Harold Rosenberg, "Tradition—or Starting from Scratch," *Art
and Other Serious Matters* (1985)

Language play releases the possibility of meaning that is
inherent in language, that is built up in it through tradition.
—Ronald Sukenick, in an interview (1981)

"Forming the habit of experimental observation," Thomas Munro writes, "one learns to adjust one's apperceptive habits to new kinds of sensory effect, new meanings and arrangements." Not only artists but the audience for art also resembles scientists in making new discoveries through experimental processes, developing perceptual capacities—powers of mind—that were previously dormant.

The aim of art in our time is the creation not of "beauty" but of rare experience; the effect of innovative art is not "pleasure" but unusual perception.

A famous fish-factor found himself father of five flirting females—
Fanny, Florence, Fernanda, Francesca, and Fenella. The first four
were flat-featured, ill-favored, forbidding-faced, freckled frumps, fretful, flippant, foolish, and flaunting. Fenella was a fine-featured, fresh,
fleet-footed fairy, frank, free, and full of fun. The fisher failed, and was
forced by fickle fortune to forego his footman, forfeit his forefathers'
fine fields, and find a forlorn farm-house in a forsaken forest. The four
fretful females, fond of figuring at feasts in feathers and fashionable
finery, fumed at their fugitive father. Forsaken by fulsome, flattering
fortune-hunters, who followed them when first they flourished, Fenella
fondled her father, flavored their food, forgot her flattering followers,
and frolicked in a frieze without flounces. The father, finding himself
forced to forage in foreign parts for a fortune, found he could afford a
faring to his five fondlings. The first four were fain to foster their frivolity
with fine frills and fans, fit to finish their father's finances; Fenella,
fearful of flooring him, formed a fancy for a full fresh flower. Fate
favored the fish-factor for a few days, when he fell in with a fog; his
faithful Filley's footsteps faltered, and food failed. He found himself in
front of a fortified fortress. Finding it forsaken, and feeling himself
feeble, and forlorn with fasting, he fed on the fish, flesh, and fowl he
found, fricasseed, and when full fell flat on the floor. Fresh n the
forenoon, he forthwith flew to the fruitful fields, and not forgetting
Fenella, he filched a fair flower; when a foul, frightful, fiendish figure
flashed forth: 'Felonious fellow, fingering my flowers, I'll finish you! Fly;
say farewell to your fine felicitous family, and face me in a fortnight!'
The faint-hearted fisher fumed and faltered, and fast and far was his
flight. His five daughters flew to fall at his feet and fervently felicitate
him. Frantically and fluently he unfolded his fate. Fenella, forthwith
fortified by filial fondness, followed her father's footsteps, and flung
her faultless form at the foot of the frighteful figure, who forgave the
father, and fell flat on his face, for he had fervently fallen in a fiery fit
of love for the fair Fenella. He feasted her till, fascinated by his
faithfulness, she forgot the ferocity of his face, form, and features, and
frankly and fondly fixed Friday, fifth of February, for the affair to come
off. There was festivity, fragrance, finery, fireworks, fricasseed frogs,
fritters, fish, flesh, fowl, and frumentry, frontignac, flip, and fare fit for
the fastidious; fruit, fuss, flambeaux, four fat fiddlers and fifers; and the
frightful form of the fortunate and frumpish fiend fell from him, and he
fell at Fenella's feet a fair-favored, fine, frank, freeman of the forest.
Behold the fruits of filial affection.   —Anonymous

INFLUENCE

Creative imitation is the surest sign of artistic influence, for imitation signifies that another artist has successfully assimilated the original creative advance. And if this happens once, it will probably happen again, each new imitation breeding the possibility of yet further imitations, as a resonant innovation eventually spreads beyond the artist's personal milieu.

By suggesting how else art might be made, the initial inventor ultimately influences how alternative art comes to be widely perceived; so that by changing the creative procedures of many artists, the successful innovator eventually revamps the sensory capacities—literally, the perceptual muscles—of an audience. Paul Cézanne and then Piet Mondrian quite literally changed how we see; Igor Stravinsky and then Edgard Varèse how we hear. What art shares with advertising is the desire to insinuate itself into audiences' heads.

In the course of its development, an artistic invention generates energies that have an impact that is often implicit, indirect, and subliminal. Harold Bloom writes in *The Anxiety of Influence* (1975), "Criticism is the art of knowing the hidden roads that go from poem to poem." No, such geography is the stuff of art history, which is a branch of intellectual history. The

A new kind of writing appears, to be greeted at first with disdain and derision; we hear that the tradition has been flouted, and that chaos has come. After a time it appears that the new way of writing is not destructive but re-creative. It is not that we have repudiated the past, as the obstinate enemies—and also the stupidest supporters—of any new movement like to believe; but that we have enlarged our conception of the past; and that in the light of what is new we see the past in a new pattern.
—T. S. Eliot, *To Criticize the Critic* (1965)

Poets influence us because we fall in love with their poems . . . . Criticism is as much a series of metaphors for the acts of loving what we have read as for the acts of reading themselves.
—Harold Bloom, *Figures of a Capable Imagination* (1976)

Every major work of art forces upon us a reassessment of all previous works of art.
—George Kubler, *The Shape of Time* (1962)

All influence is dialectical, in that it involves both gain and loss for both giver and recipient. And so all influences induce anxiety, the dread that there will be not enough for oneself, particularly of mental and spiritual space.
—Harold Bloom, *Figures of Capable Imagination* (1976)

latter can be as valuable to avant-garde scholarship as criticism, mostly because genuine influence can be a measure of worth.

Monumentally avant-garde art affects future work not only in its own genre but other arts as well. Think of all the literature reflecting cubism and the music echoing Gertrude Stein. Cross-art influence is, indeed, an implicit but sure measure of major art.

The creation of new forms in art brings recreation in life.

MACARONIC MOTHER GOOSE

JACK AND JILL

Jack cum amico Jill,
    Ascendit super montem;
Johannes cecedit down the hill,
    Ex forte fregit frontem.

LITTLE BO-PEEP

Parvula Bo-peep
Amisit her sheep,
Et nescit where to find 'em;

Desere alone,
Et venient home,
Cum omnibus caudis behind 'em.

LITTLE JACK HORNER

Parvus Jacobus Horner
Sedebat in corner,
Edens a Christmas pie;
Inferuit thumb,
Extraherit plum—
Clamans, "Quid sharp puer am I!"

—Anonymous

THE LIFE OF FORMS

Biological metaphors appropriately characterize the career of innovative forms. That is, a form is born, it grows and matures before passing through a period of senility, which presages its eventual demise. Once this process has begun, it may be opposed; but it cannot be reversed.

For literary value, naturalistic fiction is as esthetically dead as rhymed verse; Shavian theater is as indisputably dead as linear detective fiction.

Collage, which was probably the single greatest formal invention of twentieth-century art, reached its artistic demise in the nineteen-sixties. That is to say not that collage disappeared—quite the contrary is true—but that recent works indebted to collage techniques were no longer so strikingly original. What initially made collage so fertile was not just the enormous number of possibilities but its usefulness in all the arts. Once artists discovered the principle of splicing together materials that would not normally be found together, the potential for realizing pointed juxtapositions seemed limitless. As the syntax of collage became familiar, it was popularized in posters, ads, and even popular music. Almost anyone with a pair of scissors and a taste for incongruity could facilely do it.

Problems of design, of composition and balance and contrast, are obviously as central in the verbal arts as they are in music or painting.
—Northrop Frye, *The Secular Scripture* (1976)

As a general rule, I would like to add: A work of art is perceived against a background of, and by means of association with, other works of art. The form of the work of art is determined by the relation to other forms existing before it. . . . A new form appears not in order to express a new content, but in order to replace an old form, which has already lost its artistic value.
—Viktor Shklovsky, "The Connection Between Devices of *Syuzhet* Construction and General Stylistic Devices" (1919)

Human consciousness is in perpetual pursuit of a language and a style. To assume consciousness is at once to assume form. Even at levels far below the zone of definition and clarity, forms, measures, and relationships exist.
—Henri Focillon, *The Life of Forms* (1934)

Modernism presupposes an antagonism to accessibility by accentuating the analytical faculties; modernist aesthetics, for example, asserts the self-critical "task" of art. Style, on the other hand, assumes the ascendancy of familiar elements which can be easily consumed, quickly assimilated. At the point where modernist forms become a "style," modernism degenerates into mannerism.
—Daryl Chin, "Talking with Lucinda Childs" (1979)

On 30 December 1964 *Waiting for Godot* was revived at the Royal Court Theatre in London with Nicol Williamson as Vladimir. The production was extremely favorably received by the critics. As to the play—the general verdict seems to be that it was a modern classic now but had one great fault: its meaning and

However, the time came when collage devices could no longer have the capacity to generate original art; they could no longer instill the sense of awesome surprise that even sophisticated viewers experience in the presence of something new. My own estimate is that this moment occurred around 1962, not because of any historical determinism, but simply because I cannot think of a single avant-garde work, composed since then in any art, that is formally based upon collage.

The last great use of collage in poetry, for instance, occurred in Pound's *Cantos*, whose "idiogrammatic method" combines smaller images to create a larger mosaic. Innovative when Pound began it (1915), the long poem recapitulates the evolution of its primary form, becoming by its end (1970) a compendium of ways in which poetry need no longer be written. (It may also be the last example of a book-length poem sustained from beginning to end by a unique identifiable voice.) The last truly major collage in fiction was William Burroughs' *Naked Lunch* (1958); in essaying, Michael Butor's *Mobile* (1962). The last successful collages in visual art were Robert Rauschenberg's three-dimensional combines of the late 1950s.

In my temporal judgment, associational syntax in poetry is now as senile as the "confessional" voice; the first-person narrator in fic-

symbolism were a little too obvious. . . . When the same play made its first appearance in London in August 1955 it had met with a wide measure of incomprehension. Indeed, the verdict of most critics was that it was completely obscure, a farrago of pointless chit-chat.

The speed with which the incomprehensible avant-garde work turns into the all too easily understood modern classic in our epoch is astonishing and is only equalled by everyone's readiness to forget his own first reactions when confronted with works of art that break new ground.

—Martin Esslin, *The Theatre of the Absurd* (second edition, 1969)

More than any other formal device of the avant-garde, collage and its mutations (photomontage, assemblage, sampling, etc.) entered the culture at large. Collage is everywhere, from the gallery to the preschool to the high gloss ad; in this age of the putative disappearance of master narratives it is a master form in its own right. One reason for this successs is that collage is both loaded and empty: a rich formal apparatus, a compelling critique of pictorial convention, and a bank on which any number of cultural programs can be inscribed.

—Paul Mann, *The Theory Death of the Avant-Garde* (1991)

The next item, "Raman (v.d.vug zvatách s' .r'zul'.-tátm)" (A novel [in two stomachs with result]). . . has as its first page a new list of "Signs used in 'Raman'", which is partly redundant with the initial list, but adds a few explanations needed specifically for the work which takes up the second page. It is in two brief parts, or rather "stomachs", which together are to last only fifteen seconds, as indicated at the beginning of the first part. Seeming to take a cue from the preceding work, it has arches and lines linking various parts of the text and musical notation used to convey the precise pitches of specific sounds. However, the intent of these lines is unclear, nor are they explained on the preceding page.

—Gerald Janecek, "A. N. Cicerin, Constructivist Poet" (1989)

tion seems as depleted as chronological narrative; reportage of nonsequential vignettes seems as artistically inconsequential as a theater of social representation. Perhaps the surest index of spectator sophistication is the experience of discovering that something that was once shockingly original (and "unacceptable") is now utterly familiar (and, alas, acceptable).

The spectator today admiring a Braque collage appreciates it not as avant-garde art but as art history. Nothing more discredits the predominant taste in video art, as well as some 1980s painting enthusiasms, than a favoring of collage.

In art, unlike life, death is a symptom of success.

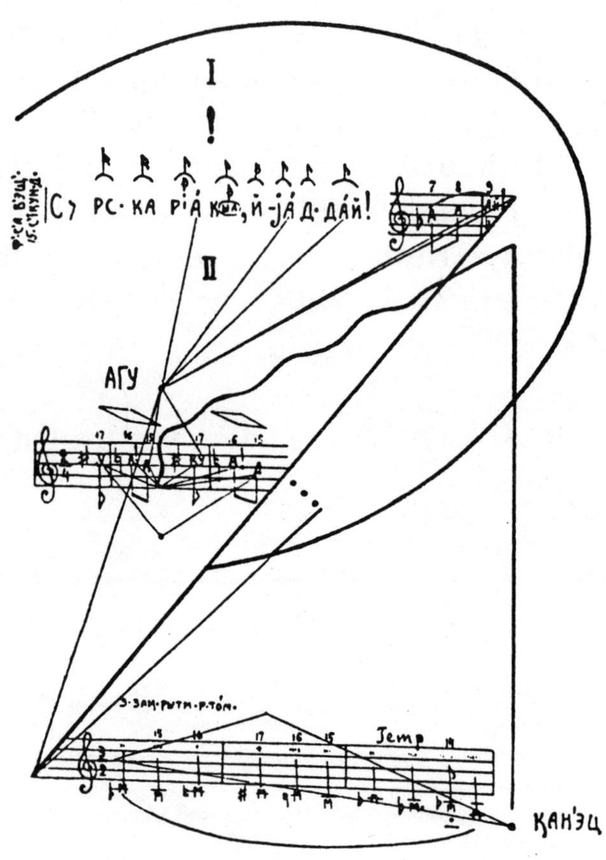

—A. N. Cicerin, from G. Janecek, "A. N. Cicerin, Constructivist Poet"

SCIENTIFIC REVOLUTIONS

One of the most inadvertently illuminating essays about avant-garde art is Thomas S. Kuhn's *The Structure of Scientific Revolutions* (1962), which implicitly provides a neat and accurate model for understanding revolutions in artistic style. As Kuhn has it, a certain paradigm dominates a scientific field at a particular time, and by *paradigm* he means "universally recognized scientific achievements that for a time provide model problems and solutions to a community of practitioners."

By analogy, representationalism in painting and diatonic tonality in music were paradigms, while rhyme and meter had a similar function in poetry. Not only do dimensions of this dominant paradigm inform all endeavors within an intellectual field; a paradigm also offers general guidelines for deploying the materials of an art.

Into a settled field (or art) comes a new work that is so radically different—so revolutionary—that it departs from, and thus conflicts with, the reigning paradigm. As Kuhn describes this process, a revolutionary work is one that "necessitated the community's rejection of one time-honored scientific theory in favor of another incompatible with it. Each produced a consequent shift in the problems available for sci-

Given any rule, however "fundamental" or "necessary" for science, there are always circumstances . . . when it is advisable to introduce, elaborate, and defend ad hoc hypotheses, or hypotheses which contradict well-established and generally accepted experimental results, or hypotheses whose content is smaller than the content of the existing and empirically adequate alternative, or self-inconsistent hypotheses, and so on.
—Paul Feyerband, *Against Method* (1975)

There has never been a science, or a new stage in the history of the different sciences, that did not in the beginning have its false creators and parasites who followed fashion and the seduction of novelty. This has been the case with all the new "schools" of linguistics, at least from the Enlightenment to the present day. In addition, every new step is characterized by purely theoretical disputes over the desirable limits of the new science.
—Roman Jakobson and Krystyna Pomorska, *Dialogues* (1980)

Now we have to make a differentiation between the craftsmen, just as you do in science between applied scientists and pure scientists. Einstein is a pure scientist. We are pure researchers in literature.
—Arlene Zekowski, quoted in *Open Letter*, 19 (Fall, 1974)

The history of any period of poetry seen from the point of view of its verse is the history of its struggle to prevent Language from becoming a new form of doggerel or—equally a hard job— to prevent an older form of language from relapsing into the basic doggerel of the mother tongue; just as, from the social point of view, it is the history of readers catching on to new rhythms or new relations between rhythm and meter. This is not a superficial but a primary interest.
—R. P. Blackmur, "Lord Tennyson's Scissors: 1912-50" (1952)

entific scrutiny and . . . each transformed the scientific imagination in ways that we shall ultimately need to describe as a transformation of the world within which scientific work was done."

In astronomy, the prototypical revolutionary was Copernicus, whose description of the universe replaced the Ptolemaic image. In modern painting, two analogies for a scientific revolution were, of course, cubism and collage; in music, two revolutions were dissonant counterpoint and Schoenberg's twelve-tone system; in poetry, free verse and then associational syntax where images and perceptions are strung together, rather than developed in a step-by-step linear fashion.

It is Kuhn's thesis that the history of science does not observe accumulative and linear models, where contributions inevitably follow upon each other. Rather, the history of each scientific field is a discontinuous series of drastic reorientations.

The histories of modern art and writing have, of course, the same structural shape, not only because every genuine artistic advance incorporates at least one prior esthetic heresy, but also because every innovation attracts, almost as a measure of its success, both a squadron of followers and an army of detractors. One reason for the similarity of histories is that both art-

The subject matter [Jasper Johns] displayed in January 1958 was different enough to precipitate a crisis in criticism. Despite a half-century of formalist indoctrination, it proved almost impossible to see the paintings for subject matter. It seemed to be the most interesting point about Johns that he mangaged somehow to discover uninteresting things to paint. An impasse for everyone. . . . Like all important original statements [his paintings] unbalanced the *status quo* and demanded an instant review of received notions.
—Leo Steinberg, *Jasper Johns* (1963)

A new form is not intelligible to everyone; many find it difficult. Perhaps. The ordinary, the banal is, of course, simpler, more pleasant, more comfortable. Euclid's world is very simple, and Einstein's world is very difficult—but it is no longer possible to return to Euclid. No revolution, no heresy is comfortable to easy. For it is a leap, it is a break in the smooth evolutionary curve, and a break is a wound, a pain. But the wound is necessary: most of mankind suffers from hereditary sleeping sickness, and victims of this sickness (entropy) must not be allowed to sleep, or it will be their final sleep, death.
—Evgeny Zamyatin, "On Literature, Revolution, Entropy, and Other Matters" (1923)

ists and scientists comprise international self-conscious communities that are based upon a good deal of professional communication, especially in the form of specialized journals. As Michael Kirby observes, "Like the scientist, the avant-garde artist is working [initially] for a very limited audience whose experience, understanding of historic developments and current concepts in the field, and interest make it possible for it to appreciate points that are unavailable to a general audience." Kirby continues elsewhere, "In art as in science, it is the new that gives the field its significance."

The arts do not evolve in the sense of becoming more complex or more refined, or in building progressively upon prior achievements; but change indeed they do. Nonetheless, change in art has no more direction, ultimately no more "progress," than change in science.

Was it Baudelaire who said that the chief task of artistic genius is the invention of a new paradigm?

We lived beneath the mat
    Warm and snug and fat
            But one woe, + that
                    Was the cat!
                        To our joys
                        a clog, In
                        our eyes a
                    fog, On our
                hearts a log
            Was the dog!
        When the
    cat's away,
    Then
    the mice
    will
    play,
        But, alas!
            one day, (So they say)
                Came the dog and
                    cat, Hunting
                        for a
                        rat,
                    Crushed
                    the mice
                all flat,
                Each
                one
                as
                he
                sat
                Underneath the mat, Warm+snug+
                fat - Think of that!

—Lewis Carroll, "Mouse Tail"

AUTONOMY OF ART

It was a radical innovation of modernism to regard art as primarily about art and only incidentally about something else, and every genuine avant-garde in our time has endeavored to refine this peculiarly modernist understanding.

Modern art thus exists in a domain decisively apart not just from previous art but from human life as well, just as contemporary scholarship inhabits yet another predominantly autonomous domain. What art and scholarship also have in common is that they are collective enterprises whose achievements and traditions survive individual births and deaths.

As each new work of art is primarily about matters that belong exclusively to Art, it is only incidentally about life, just as life is primarily about Life and only incidentally about Art. "Feelings" belong to Life; "forms" to Art.

"A painter is in love with painting, not scenery," Ad Reinhardt wrote. "Art comes from art and artists and art history." Artists descend from other artists, in part because the desire to become a professional artist is usually inspired by an enticing image of the artistic activity. (For me it began with reading Sinclair Lewis when I was fourteen and thinking that writing is something I'd like to do myself.)

Poetry can only be made out of other poems; novels out of other novels. Literature shapes itself, and is not shaped externally: the *forms* of literature can no more exist outside literature than the forms of sonata and fugue can exist outside music.
—Northrop Frye, *Anatomy of Criticism* (1957)

A painter needs but recall his first paintings, or a poet his first poems, to realize that they served him as a means of participating not in the world of men, but in that of art, and what he asked of them was less a conquest of the world of reality, an escape from it, or even an expression of it, than a sense of fellowship with brother artists. . . . The world of art is not an idealized world but *another world;* thus every artist feels himself akin to the musical composer.
—André Malraux, *The Imaginary Museum* (1953)

Ultimately a plastic work has to be judged by its plastic. Its goodness or badness of the combined curves and straights, etc., masses, combinations, or same, etc., will be a matter of their form and even their expressiveness will depend upon this and not on what the sculptor says he intended to express.
—Ezra Pound, "Epstein, Religion and Meaning" (1930)

Aesthetic programs have replaced regional masterpieces as authority and as inspiration. "Every modern activity," said Paul Valery, "is dominated and governed by *myths* in the form of *ideologies*" (his italics). The roots of contemporary creation lie not in observations of nature nor in earlier works of art but in theoretical interpretations of these.
—Harold Rosenberg, "Criticism and Its Premises" (1975)

Most "philosophy" in our time is primarily about the intellectual enterprise bearing that name and secondarily about Life, for each new work of philosophy is designed initially to comment upon issues defined within that intellectual field. A new philosophical idea is, like a new painting, valued primarily for its contribution to a conscious tradition of professional concern and only incidentally for its relevance to common experience. Every acknowledged field/art has not only a tradition but a logic that innovative work at once extends and redirects. As *forms* are the stuff of Art, so *methodologies* are the basis of scholarship.

Just as a painter does not learn how to paint, or even how to represent the scene before his eyes, until he sees (and studies) other paintings, so no one knows how to write until he has read plenty of previous writing; and no one knows how to "do" philosophy until he has extensively studied prior philosophy, whether in school or on his own.

Certain Dadaists, among other artists, claimed to put "life" above art, but the most tangible survivors of their counter-conventional effort have been examples of innovative art. When Marcel Duchamp purportedly "abandoned art for life," his decision had meaning only within the traditions of visual art; everyday Life went merrily along, unaffected. Only a commu-

It is the critic's task, in every age, to fight for the autonomy of the arts, and never under any circumstances allow himself to be seduced into judging the arts, positively or negatively, by their attachments.
—Northrop Frye, "Criticism, Visible and Invisible" (1964)

In painting and sculpture we experience the form alone for its own sake and even create a new one, independent of a long extinct creed which held true for a given cult; the very construction of form is for us an abstract "drug" enabling us to experience metaphysical feelings. We maintain that likewise there must be the possibility of a similar form in the theatre, a form in which becoming through time, the simple fact of something "happening" defined only in a purely formal way—the elements of which will of course be human actions—will be able, independent of the real-life content of the actions themselves and of the consistency of characterization of the characters who act, to usher us into a dimension of experience totally different from real life, into the sphere of metaphysical feelings, as it is in pure form.
—Stanislaw Ignacy Witkiewicz, "The Analogy with Painting," Introduction to *The Theory of Pure Form in the Theatre* (1920).

Art is art. Everything else is everything else.
—Ad Reinhardt, "25 Lines of Words on Art: Statement" (1958)

Our respect is not for the subject-matter but for the creative power of the artist; for that which he is capable of adding to his subject from himself; or, in fact, his capability to dispense with external subjects altogether, to create from himself or from elements.

    We hold that life has its own satisfactions and that after a man has lived life up to the hilt, he should still have sufficient energy to go on to the satisfactions of art, which are different

nity of artistically knowledgeable people can distinguish, or be persuaded to distinguish, No-Art, or Ex-Art, or Un-Art from Life.

Most artists will claim, when prompted, to make a contribution to our understanding of life; but what we value, especially in historical perspective, is their discoveries about Art. Developments in pure mathematics are yet more explicitly subsumed within the discipline's own traditions.

Drastic changes in society inspire radicals to make political action and poets to write poems, each responding to social impetus with energy to make his or her own "art." One competence that both of them have learned, in mastering their respective media of communication, is the possibility of optimal response to outside influences.

What is most valuable in a poem is not its "message" but qualities indigenous to poetry. The success of its communication depends upon both the reader's and the writer's love and intelligence, less of life than of Poetry. In approaching a new work of literature, we bring to it "all of our experience," which, as a measure of our literacy, includes a good deal of reading.

When content is more important than mediumistic qualities (or the relationship between them), then the reader is perceiving the work not as literature but as something else—as

from the satisfactions of life. I still now say loftily: they are beyond it. The satisfactions of art differ from the satisfactions of life as the satisfactions of seeing differ from the satisfactions of hearing. There is no need to dispense with either. The artist who has no "ideas about art," like the man who has no ideas about life, is a dull dog.
—Ezra Pound, *Gaudier-Brzeska* (1916)

All writing is a demonstration of method; it can assume a method or investigate it. In this sense, style and mode are always at issue, for all styles are socially mediated conventions open to reconvening at any time.
—Charles Bernstein, "Writing and Method" (1983)

An avant-garde in art advances art-as-art or it isn't an avant-garde.
—Ad Reinhardt, unpublished notes (1962-63)

history, as sociology, as psychology, or as reportage. Ultimately, the direct representation of reality belongs not to Literature but to something else.

Language exists for artists not for the expression of personality but as material embodying not only denotations and connotations but yet other potentialities that have been scarcely explored. An avant-garde writer makes discoveries about language, or his relationship to language; discoveries about oneself belong in a diary.

Every work of imaginative writing incorporates, as a principal *meaning,* certain notions about literature; it embodies *insight* into issues of appropriateness and possibilities in literary art. A new piece of writing is more valuable and praiseworthy if these generic ideas are original and suggestive. Literature, unlike journalism, survives not by "saying something new," but by inventing something not seen before and thus by enhancing the corpus of literary experience.

Formal ideas generate works of art; content fills them. Every work draws a circle around itself, letting the reader know what does (and does not) belong to it. All writing is hermetic to idiosyncratic degrees—writers writing what can only be written. The idea of art's autonomy is profoundly liberating, if only because esthetic experience at its truest depends upon personal

The Broken English Dream   Sueño en inglés goleta

I

••••••••••••••••••••
••••••••••••••••••
••••••••••••••••••
••••••••••••••••••

•••••••••••••••••••••
••••••••••••••••••
•••••••••••••••••••••
•••••••••••••••

•••••••••••••••••
••••••••••••••••••
••••••••••••••••
•••••••••••••••••••••

•••••••••••••••••
••••••••••••••••••
••••••••••••••
•••••••••••••••••••••

II

???????????????????????
???????????????????
?????????????????????????
?????????????????????

??????????????????????????
??????????????????????
??????????????????????????
???????????????????

I

••••••••••••••••••••
.........!!......l
••••••••••••••••••••
.........!!......l

••••••••••••••••••••
........!!......l
••••••••••••••••••••
........!!......l

!......!!.........
••••••••••••••••••••••
!......!!.........
••••••••••••••••••••••

!......!!.........
••••••••••••••••••••••
!......!!.........
••••••••••••••••••••••

(Traducción: Alfredo Mat

II

???????????????????????
???????????????????
??????????????????????????
••••••••••••••••••

???????????????????????
?????? ???????????
????????? ?????? ??
???????????????????

—Pedro Pietri, from *The Puerto Rican Poets* (1972)

and cultural freedom. (Anyone who has ever lived
in a totalitarian culture knows in his or her gut
the importance of this last truth.)

,,,,,,,,,,,,,,,,,,,,,,,
,,,,,,,,,,,,,,,,,,
,,,,,,,,,,,,,,,,,,,,,
,,,,,,,,,,,,,,,,,

,,,,,,,,,,,,,,,,
,,,,,,,,,,,,,,,,,,,,
,,,,,,,,,,,,,,,
,,,,,,,,,,,,,,,,,,,,,

,,,,,,,,,,,,,,,,,,,,,,
,,,,,,,,,,,,,,,,,,
,,,,,,,,,,,,,,,,,,, ,
,, ,,,,,,,,,,,,,,

,,,,,,,,,,,,,,,,,,,,,
,,,,,,,,,,,,,,,,,
,,,,,,,,,,,,,,,,,,,,,
:

(Traducción: Ellen G. Matilla)

III

•••••••••••••••••
,,,,,,,,,,,,,,,,,,,,,,,
•••••••••••••••••
,,,,,,,,,,,,,,,,,,,,,,

•••••••••••••••••••
,,,,,,,,,,,,,,,,,,,,,,
•••••••••••••••••
,,,,,,,,,,,,,,,,,,,,,

••••••••••••••••••
,,,,,,,,,,,,,,,,,,,,,,,
•••••••••••••••••
,,,,,,,,,,,,,,,,,,,,,,

III

•••••••••••••••••
,,,,,,,,,,,,,,,,,,,,,,,
•••••••••••••••••
,,,,,,,,,,,,,,,,,,,,,,

•••••••••••••••••
,,,,,,,,,,,,,,,,,,,,
,,,,,,,,,,,,,,,,,,,,,,
•••••••••••••••••
••••••••••••••••••••
,,,,,,,,,,,,,,,,,,,,,,,

•••••••••••••••••
,,,,,,,,,,,,,,,,,,,,,,
•••••••••••••••••
,,,,,,,,,,,,,,,,,,,,,,,

••••••••••••••••••
,,,,,,,,,,,,,,,,,,,
,,,,,,,,,,,,,,,,,,,,,,
•••••••••••••••••
••••••••••••••••••••
,,,,,,,,,,,,,,,,,,,,,,,

(Traducción: Alfredo Matilla)

—Pedro Pietri, from *The Puerto Rican Poets* (1972)

"EXPERIENCE"

This difference between Art and Life explains why it is largely by reading, rather than "living," that one learns not only how to write but how to understand what has been written. What distinguishes the writer from the non-writer is, first, his extensive experience with written forms and then his capacity to fabricate mountains of literature out of molehills in life. And what distinguishes the literate reader from the nonliterate is his capacity to accept the mountains as worth his climb.

Rather than speak of literature as "experience mediated by language," to quote a common platitude, why not regard it as literary language mediated by experience, which includes, of course, a extensive familiarity with literary works.

Technical invention (or distinction) and moral perception, if present together, theoretically make a work better than one without the other; but the second without the first is, in thrust, closer to preaching than to art.

This separation of Art from Life also accounts for such contradictions and contrasts as why an artist can succeed in art, while failing in life (or vice versa), or why he may show integrity in art and opportunism in life, courage in his profession and cowardice in life, or why he may seem vibrant in life and dead in art, or intelligent

You can have the most interesting inner life in the world and not be able to produce an interesting poem, and you can have a seemingly bland inner life—whatever that may be—and produce the most beautiful poems in the world. It's not a question of your inner life, it's a question of what you're writing . . . alas.
—Charles Bernstein, "Socialist Realism or Real Socialism?" (1981)

There is a shallow test which holds that the original poet goes direct to life, and the derivative poet to 'literature.' When we look into the matter, we find that the poet who is really 'derivative' is the poet who *mistakes* literature for life, and very often the reason why he makes this mistake is that he had not read enough.
—T. S. Eliot, "Ezra Pound" (1928)

Most poetry is on commonplace themes, and the freshness, what the poet supplies, is in the language. There are other matters of importance in original poetry, but it is the freshness of Mr. Pound's language, not the power of his mind or of a sounder interpretation, that makes his translations excellent poetry.
—R. P. Blackmur, "Masks of Ezra Pound" (1934)

The imagination is an actual force comparable to electricity or steam, it is not a plaything but a power that has been used from the first to raise the understanding of—it is not necessary to resort to mysticism—In fact it is this which has kept back the knowledge I seek—The value of the imagination to the writer consists in its ability to make words. Its unique power is to give created forms reality, actual existence.
—William Carlos Williams, *Spring and All* (1923)

in art and stupid in life, or egomaniacal in his art and yet modest and generous in life, or eccentric in art and conventional in life. The possibilities for discrepancy are limitless.

Biographies of artists are irrelevant unless they focus upon how it was that Art, rather than something else, was produced by idiosyncratic creative methods. What makes Hemingway special was not the life he led but his linguistic discoveries and how he realized them, and how he managed, amidst distractions, to write his books. Shouldn't Faulkner's biographer be able to tell us what was on Faulkner's mind when he was writing his most distinctive sentences? And what exactly did Gertrude Stein think she was doing when she was doing it?

Just as new Art comes largely out of past Art, so new Life is primarily derived from previous Life.

SCHERTZ VOM FLACHS-NUTZE

Gewiss, der liebe Flachs ist gar ein nützes wesen;
Der, der es wo nicht glaubt, mag diese Reime lesen:
Ein Mägdlein gieng zu Stuhl und thät, ich weiss nicht was,
Da war das Hembd ihr gut, sonts wär sie noch wol nass.
—Friedrich von Logau (1604-55)

Kikakokú!
Ekoraláps!

Wîso kollipánda opolôsa.
Ipasátta îh fûo.
Kikakokú proklínthe petêth.
Nikifilí mopaléxio intipáschi benakáffro—própsa
   pî! própsa pî!
Jasóllu nosaressa flípsei.
Aukarótto passakrússar Kikakokú.
Núpsa púsch?
Kikakokú bulurú?
Futupúkke—própsa pî!
Jasóllu . . . . . .
—Paul Scheerbart (1897)

CONSTRUCTIVISM

Two polarities of artistic creativity are expressionism and constructivism, each term defining a different attitude toward the making of imaginative things. In the former, the artist thinks he is primarily "expressing" himself, even though he is also using forms and materials that exist apart from himself. Allen Ginsberg, for instance, regards his poetry as "GRAPHING the movement of the mind on the page." A further assumption is that, to quote Ginsberg again, "If the poet's mind is shapely, his art will be shapely." *Surrealism* is an extreme extension of expressionism.

The constructivist artist believes, by contrast, that he is building things apart from himself, even though his creations are liable to reveal certain personal proclivities. As Piet Mondrian, himself a scrupulous constructivist, explained the difference, "One aims at the *direct creation of universal beauty,* the other at the *aesthetic expression of oneself.*"

Both constructivism and expressionism represent modernist advances over representational/reportorial art.

In the history of painting, what distinguished cubism from constructivism was the former's lingering interests in mundane reality (restructured, to be sure) and the expression of an attitude toward it, while constructivism emphasized the presentation of invented forms. Thus, constructivist paintings are generally geometric and nonmimetic. In sculpture, the term *constructivism* customarily refers to objects that are constructed, rather than

I believe that life is indestructible, and the force that makes it indestructible is human constructive consciousness. . . . Art is an effort of our consciousness directed toward a specific goal—to know and to make known, to give shape to the shapeless, structure to the decomposed, and to lend form to the amorphous origin of chaos.
—Naum Gabo, *Of Divers Arts* (1962)

Much as I respect the individual touch it must have no personal element.
—El Lissitzky.

Instead of this universe of "signification" (psychological, social, functional), we must try, then, to construct a world both more solid and more immediate. Let it be first of all by their *presence* that objects and gestures establish themselves, and let this presence continue to prevail over whatever explanatory theory that may try to enclose them in a system of references, whether emotional, sociological, Freudian, or metaphysical.
—Alain Robbe-Grillet, "A Future for the Novel" (1956)

In European art during the early years of this century, the nonfigurative movements, such as Constructivism, Suprematism, Neoplasticism, and the Bauhaus, which were concerned with pure abstraction, had as a common denominator a rigorous formal rationalism. Their fundamental invention was to translate into visual terms the rational consciousness of the world, so that form should express the logic of the hidden structure of reality.
—Italo Tomassoni, *Mondrian* (1969)

cast or carved.

Dada is in retrospect essentially an inversion of constructivism, turning its positive stance upside down for laudably perverse cultural ends.

The constructivist assumes that, to quote Mondrian again, "It is possible to express oneself profoundly and humanly by plastics alone." To put it differently, in visual material itself can be discovered all the profundity and humanity that art is capable of expressing. The individual character of the work comes from qualities of esthetic style, rather than personality. The poet is not an ingredient in the poem but a chef cooking the available ingredients. The constructivist artist is, in essence, the guy who moves the stuff around.

Here and elsewhere, esthetic decisions as such have ethical implications.

Mondrian thought that constructivist art revealed the essence of the universe, but his claim defies the empiricism entwined in the constructivst attitude.

One primary quality distinguishing recent avant-garde writing from its predecessors is constructivist developments new to the history of literature.

Every writer, if he develops at all, develops either outwards into society and history using wider and more material of that sort, or he develops inwards into imagination and beyond that into spirit, using perhaps no more external material than before and maybe even less but deepening it and making it operate in many different inner dimensions until it opens up perhaps the religious or holy basis of the whole thing.

—Ted Hughes, in an interview, *Works in Progress* (1971)

For there *is* a fundamental value of modern art, and one that goes far deeper than a mere quest of the pleasure of the eye. Its annexation of the visible world was but a preliminary move, as it stands for that immemorial impulse of creative art: the desire to build up a world apart and self-contained, existing in its own right: a desire which, for the first time in the history of art, has become the be-all and the end-all of the artist. That is why our modern masters paint their pictures as the artists of ancient civilization carved or painted gods.

—André Malraux, *The Imaginary Museum* (1953)

STYLISTIC PLURALISM

In each art today, there exists not one avant-garde but several, each of which stands decisively beyond earlier stylistic positions. The contemporary pursuit of possibility allows the development of numerous alternative positions, rather than just a single one; for at the root of the modernist awakening is an acknowledgment of cultural opportunity and diversity.

One social fact making this pluralism possible is the increased number of practitioners in every art. A second factor is the existence of several avant-garde traditions within each art. In literature, for instance, there is a line of linguistic invention whose modern English language exemplars include Gertrude Stein, E. E. Cummings, Hugh MacDiarmid (in his Scots dialect poems), and James Joyce (especially in *Finnegans Wake*).

An entirely different avant-garde tradition has emphasized structural alternatives, organizing the materials of literature in unprecedented ways—Joyce again (especially in *Ulysses*), Pound, Faulkner, Stein (in her plays especially), and Samuel Beckett.

Another tradition is defined by the incorporation of materials previously regarded as nonliterary, such as the meaningless sounds of Alexei Kruchonyk's poetry, the alphabetical con-

Coffee, cough, glass, spoon, white, singing. Choose, selection, visible, lightning, garden, conversation, ink, spending, light space, morning, celebration, invisible, reception, hour, glass, curving, summons, sparkle, suffering the minisection, sanctioning the widening, less than the wireless, more certain. All the change. Any counselling non consuming and split splendor.

Forward and a rapidity and no resemblance no more utterly. Safe light, more safes no more safe for the separation.
—Gertrude Stein, "IIIIIIIIII," *Geography and Plays* (1922)

dyr bul shchyl

ubeshshchur

skum

vy so bu

r l e'z

Here Kruchenykh introduced what later was to become known as *zaum*, the so-called transrational language, of which he would become one of the main practitioners and theoreticians . . . . The poem begins with energetic monosyllables, some of which slightly resemble Russian or Ukranian words, followed by a three-syllable word of shaggy appearance. The next word looks like a fragment of some word, and the two final lines are occupied with syllables and just plain letters, respectively, the poem ending on a queer, non-Russian sounding syllable.
—Vladimir Markov, *Russian Futurism* (1968)

vention of the encyclopedia, the pictorialism of the visual poets, or the mathematical formulas in Alfred Jarry's "The Surface of God":

> —Let us note, in fact, that according to
> the formula
> $$\infty - 0 - a + a + 0 = \infty$$
> the length a is nil, so that a is not a line but a point. Therefore, *definitively* GOD IS THE TANGENTIAL POINT BETWEEN ZERO AND INFINITY

for there are no limits upon the materials available to literary creators.

It would be false to say that just one of these avant-garde traditions was necessarily more important or more "valid" or more fertile than the others, for all of them remain consequential. Not only do certain recent literary works make decisive advances within each of these strains, but some contribute to two traditions; a rare few, to all three.

These traditions remain perceptibly separate, each circumscribing not only a distinctly different way of generating (and appreciating) literary invention but a different way of understanding literature.

The avant-garde thus fights several battles on several fronts. One measure of sophisticated esthetic comprehension today is recognition of the total terrain.

—Anonymous, "Love Knot" (1600s)

Any "critical theory" attempting to govern the interpretation of particular texts with a general theory belongs to theology (or totalitarian politics) and not to the criticism of avant-garde art.

TITLE-PAGE FOR A BOOK OF EXTRACTS FROM MANY AUTHORS

Astonishing Anthology from Attractive Authors.
Broken Bits from Bulky Brains.
Choice Chunks from Chaucer to Channing.
Dainty Devices from Diverse Directions.
Echoes of Eloquence from Emiment Essayists.
Fragrant Flowers from Fields of Fancy.
Gems of Genius Gloriously Garnished.
Handy Helps from Head and Heart.
Illustrious Intellects Intelligently Interpreted.
Jewels of Judgment and Jets of Jocularity.
Kindlings to Keep from the King to the Kitchen.
Loosened Leaves from Literary Laurels.
Magnificent Morsels from Mighty Minds.
Numerous Nuggets from Notable Noodles.
Oracular Opeinions Officiously offered.
Prodigious Points from Powerful Pens.
Quirks and Quibbles from Queer Quarters.
Rare Remarks Ridiculously Repeated.
Suggestive Squibs from Sundry Sources.
Tremendous Thoughts on Thundering Topics.
Utterances from Uppermost for Use and Unction.
Valuable Views in Various Voices.
Wisps of Wit in a Wilderness of Words.
Xcellent Xtracts Xactly Xpressed.
Yawnings and Yearnings for Youthful Yankees.
Zeal and Zest from Zoroaster to Zimmerman.

—Anonymous

POUND'S APHORISMS

What is at present most valuable in Pound's *ABC* is not its argument, the battle for modernist literature, which has been won and then surpassed, but his professional example as a full-time person of letters (in an age of hobbyists and academic parttimers) and then those sentences that have continuing relevance:

Great literature is simply language charged with meaning to the utmost possible degree.

Literature is news that STAYS news.

The sum of human wisdom is not contained in any one language, and no single language is capable of expressing all forms and degrees of human comprehension.

Virgil was the official literature of the middle ages, but "everybody" went on reading Ovid.

Artists are the antennae of the race.

It is difficult to read the same detective story twice.

Much of the *permanence* of Mr. Pound's criticism is due simply to his having seen so clearly what needed to be said at a particular time; his occupation with his own moment and its needs had led him to say many things which are of permanent value, but the value of which may not be immediately appreciated by later readers who lack the sense of historical situation.

[He] has always been, first and foremost, a teacher and campaigner. He has always been impelled, not merely to find out for himself how poetry should be written, but to pass on the benefit of his discoveries to others; not simply to make these benefits available, but to insist upon their being received.
—T. S.Eliot, introduction to *The Literary Essays of Ezra Pound* (1954)

When [a professional art educator] started his art department, they found *artists* whom they brought into the university and they produced a generation of MFAs. The next thing was they got rid of the visiting artists, and they hired the MFAs, so the second generation was taught by the MFAs. The first generation of MFAs had been taught by artists, but the second generation of MFAs was taught by MFAs. So the standards kept going down. That is, I think, a description of what has ruined teaching in our art departments, the requirement of administrations for degree-holding faculty. By this time nobody hires an artist any more, and they have established the kind of approach to art which comes out of a university, not out of artists' studios.
—Harold Rosenberg, "What Is Art?" (1978)

Pound, of course, was a "difficult" poet who adored allusions. In many ways he—like the Eliot of *The Waste Land*—wrote a poetry of quotation, drawing on world literature with the adventurousness of an amateur reader.
—Jay Parini, introduction to *The Columbia History of American Poetry* (1993)

In all cases one test will be, "could this material have been made more efficient in some other medium?" You can spot the bad critic when he starts by discussing the poet and not the poem.

Any general statement is like a cheque drawn on a bank. Its value depends upon what is there to meet it. . . . In writing, a man's "name" is his reference. He has, after a time, credit.

The student having studied geometry and physics or chemistry knows that in one you begin with simple forms, in another with simple substances.

What the expert is tired of today the public will be tired of tomorrow.

The honest critic must be content to find VERY LITTLE contemporary work worth serious attention; but he must also be ready to recognize that little, and to demote work of the past when a new work surpasses it.

From the empiric angle, verse usually has some element roughly fixed and some other that varies, but which element is to be fixed and which varied, and to what degrees, is the affair of the author.

[Ezra Pound] has the most conical hodpiece of confusianisst
heronim and that chuchuffuous chinchin of his is like a footsey
kungoloo around Taishantyland.

—James Joyce, *Finnegans Wake* (1939)

MAJOR INNOVATIONS

The major esthetic innovations of recent art extend from three generative principles: minimalism, overload, and intermedia. The first term refers to the principle of reducing the amount of surface content in a work—a painting with only one color, say, or a sculpture entirely of smooth rectangular shapes, or fictions with very few words, or a poem with a severely limited vocabulary.

The contrary motive of overload informs such serial compositions as Milton Babbitt's *Relata I* (1964), which presents an awesomely large number of discrete musical events in remarkably few minutes; or an enclosed space (*aka* an environment) with an abundance of stimuli; or James Joyce's *Finnegans Wake*, where several stories, in several languages, are rendered on a single page. Reduction and elaboration, though superfically opposite, are similar in one respect: Both techniques attempt to transcend the range of time/space scales of traditional work, thereby making the listener or reader more aware of alternative perceptual durations in art.

Since experimental artists are continually trying to eschew the familiar messages of artistic communication—e.g., not only how much plot but how many characters (and pages) a "novel," say, should contain—the most interesting art of

The Minimalists appear to have realized, finally, that the far-out in itself has to be the far-out as end in itself, and that this means the furthest-out and nothing short of that. They appear also to have realized that the most original and furthest-out art of the last hundred years always arrived looking at first as though it had parted company with everything previously known as art. In other words, the furthest-out usually lay on the borderline between art and non-art.

—Clement Greenberg, "Recentness of Sculpture" (1967)

1

black   black
stone   stone

white   white
stone   stone

black   black
stone   stone

white   white
stone   stone

white   white
stone   stone

black   black
stone   stone

white   white
stone   stone

black   black
stone   stone

—Robert Lax

the past two decades tends to be either much more, or much less, than works of art used to be. While the British writer J. G. Ballard frequently compresses enough material for a novel into a fiction the length of a short story, Samuel Beckett's novels, on another hand, have progressively fewer events; and the American poet Robert Lax creates in *Black & White* (1966) an extended poem composed of only four different words (three of which are announced in the title), punctuated only by white space. Isn't the ideal of a one-page "novel" as valid and as exciting as a fiction of ten thousand pages?

Similarly, Picasso is envied for a career of fabricating so much art and Duchamp for producing so little in nearly as many years; for diametrically opposite reasons, both men successfully disrupted the expectation of art's audience.

Intermedia, the third generative principle, is an encompassing term referring to the new art forms which were invented by disjunctively marrying the materials and concepts of one traditional genre with another or others (in contrast to opera where the media consciously complement) or by integrating art itself with something previously considered nonartistic. Out of the mating of theater with painting, sculpture, music and/or dance came that art called "happenings" or "mixed-means events," while sculptures that incorporate an operational technology

Literature seems to be intermediate between music and painting: its words form patterns which approach a musical sequence
of sounds at one of its boundaries, and form patterns which
approach the hieroglyphic or pictorial image at the other. The
attempt to get as near to these boundaries as possible form the
main body of what is called experimental writing.
—Northrop Frye, "The Archetypes of Literature" (1951)

Typographical artifices worked out with great audacity have the
advantage of bringing to life a visual lyricism which was always
unknown before our age. These artifices can still go much
further and achieve the synthesis of the arts, of music, painting
and literature.
—Guillaume Apollinaire, "The New Spirit and the Poets" (1918)

With the breakdown of classical harmonies following the introduction of 'irrational' or nonharmonic juxtaposition, the Cub-
ists tacitly opened a path of infinity. Once foreign matter was
introduced into the picture in the form of paper, it was only a
matter of time before everything else foreign to paint and
canvas would be allowed to get into the creative act, including
real space.
—Allan Kaprow, *Assemblage, Environments & Happenings* (1966)

within the art, rather than as an anterior tool, comprise a genre that I call "artistic machines."

In literature, out of the melding of language with design came what is called *visual poetry* or *word-imagery,* where the enhancing coherence of words is pictorial (rather than syntactical), while *sound poetry* or *text-sound art* comes from inventively integrating musical values with initially verbal material. Since the possibilities of literary intermedia have scarcely been explored, it is reasonable to suspect that this may be the single greatest esthetic invention for our time— the sole contemporary peer of cubism and collage.

Renato Poggioli suggests that "The term avant-garde seems more appropriate to describe an invention than a discovery."

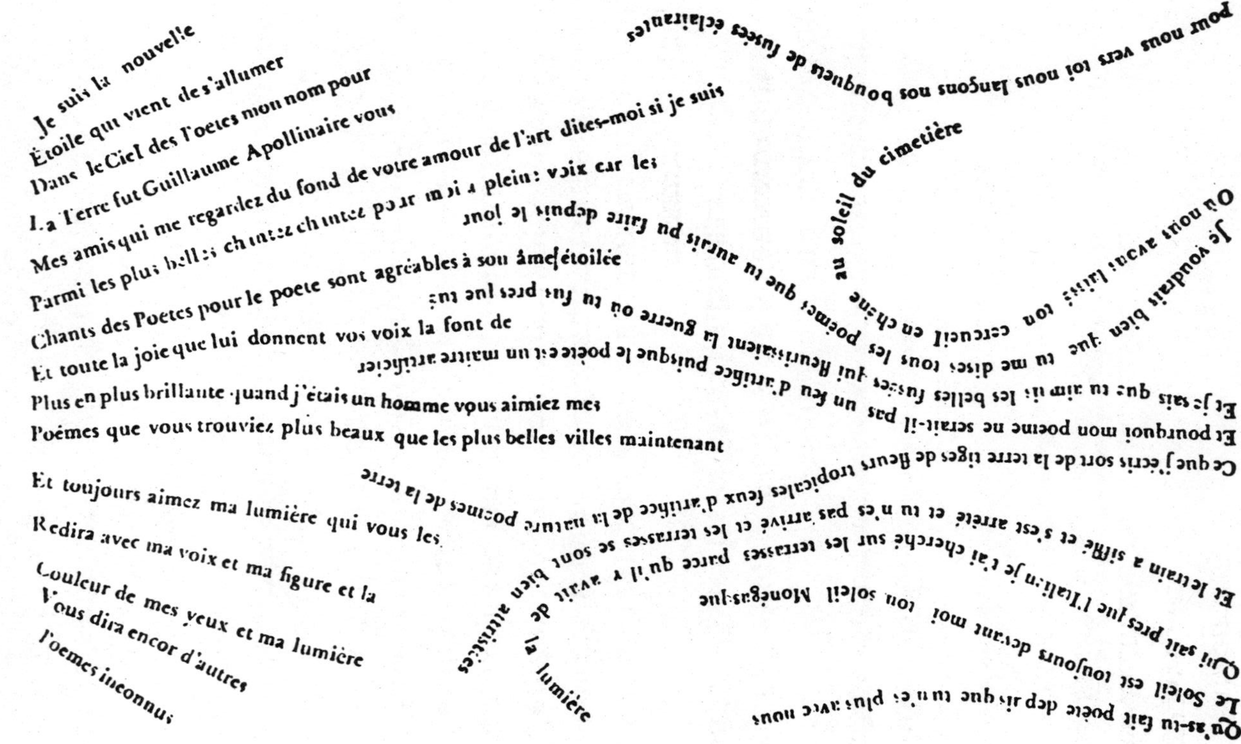

—Pierre Albert-Birot, "Offrande"

"DECLINE"

What is perceived to be "the decline of the novel," say, should not be blamed upon the absence of invention; in fiction, as in the other literary arts, the avant-garde tradition survives. Nor can this purported decline be blamed upon the diminution of an audience for fiction, for not only do Americans buy more best-selling tripe than ever before, but the sales of, say, Samuel Beckett, John Barth, and Saul Bellow indicate a larger audience for what is commonly perceived to be "serious literary fiction."

The alleged "decline of the novel" is really based, first, upon the fact that almost all novels published today patently resemble previous novels, if not in content then surely in form, and second upon the sense that too many new novels take their cues not from the intrinsic possibilities of literature but from the clichés of other media. When novels try to imitate film or are written primarily to be "taken by the movies," the medium's independence and initiative are severely compromised.

On the other hand, the reported "decline of the short story" can be attributed, quite clearly, to the decrease in the number of media publishing it. At a time when more stories are written than ever before (thanks largely to courses in "fiction writing"), fewer appear in print. Here, as else-

For well over a hundred years each successive generation has
seemed to many of its members to contain within itself the seeds
of the immanent destruction, not only of a musical tradition, but
possibly of music itself.
—Roger Sessions,"Problems and Issues Facing the Composer Today" (1960)

The title of this book announces its argument, which holds that
a panoply of growing forces and festering symptoms forecast
the likely end of 'intelligentwriting' or 'literature' as we have
known those traditions. The reason for this crisis is not that
such writing is no longer produced—quite the contrary is true—
or that it is not read—also untrue—but that the channels of
communication between intelligent writer and intelligent reader
have become so clogged and corrupted.
—Richard Kostelanetz, *The End of Intelligent Writing* (1974)

where, cultural commentators are continually
blaming art and artists for failures that are
clearly caused by machinations in the intermediary agencies.

If you want to make a personal artistic
statement, it would be wise to avoid familiar
ground; if you want commercial success, bury
your head (and heart and soul) in it.

PRINCE CHARLES PROTECTED
BY FLORA MACDONALD

All ardent acts affright an Age abased
By brutal broils, by braggart bravery braced.
Craft's cankered courage changed Culloden's cry;
"Deal deep" deposed "deal death"—"decoy," "defy:"
Enough. Ere envy enters England's eyes,
Fancy's false future fades, for Fortune flies.
Gaunt, gloomy, guarded, grappling giant griefs,
Here, hunted hard, his harassed heart he heaves;
In impious ire incessant ills invests,
Judging Jove's jealous judgments, jaundiced jests!
Kneel, kirtled knight! keep keener kingcraft known,
Let larger lore life's levelling lessons loan:
Marauders must meet malefactors' meeds;
No nation noisy non-conformists needs.
O oracles of old! our orb ordain
Peace's possession—Plenty's palmy plain!
Quiet quixotic quests; quell quarrelling;
Rebuke red riot's resonant rifle ring.
Slumber seems strangely sweet since silence smote
The threatening thunders throbbing through their
  throat.
Usurper! under uniform unwont
Vail valor's vaguest venture, vainest vaunt.
Well wot we which were wise. War's wildfire won
Ximenes, Xerxes, Xavier, Xenophon:
Yet you, ye yearning youth, *your* young years yield
Zuinglius' zealot zest—Zinzendorf zion-zealed.
—Anonymous

DIVERGENT AVANT-GARDES

What is innovative in art today tends either to purify the traditional properties of a medium or to miscegenate with other media. In painting, for one, the first motive was epitomized by Ad Reinhardt, who regarded himself as doing "pure painting," uncontaminated by motives and materials indigenous to the other arts. A recent exemplar of the second, contrary tendency has been Robert Rauschenberg, who has incorporated mundane materials, three-dimensional objects, and even operational technologies into his paintings.

In avant-garde literature, the motive of mediumistic purification tends to predominate today, in part because fewer writers than, say, painters are especially responsive to arts other than their own. Writers working in this purifying way try to engage the particular nature of their chosen medium and thus create works that cannot be easily translated into any other medium:

Poetry that cannot be set to music,

Theatrical experience that is not susceptible to filming or televising,

Novels that have no life beyond the page of print,

Poems that are not prose and cannot be facilely paraphrased.

Language constructions unified and enhanced in terms other than syntax.

Not satisfied with the suggestion through paint of our other senses, we shall utilize the specific substances of sight, sound, movement, people, odor, touch. Objects of every sort are materials for the new art: paint, chairs, food, electric and neon lights, smoke, water, old socks, a dog, movies, a thousand other things which will be discovered by the present generation of artists. Not only will these bold creators show us, as if for the first time, the world we have always had about us but ignored, but they will disclose entirely unheard-of happenings and events, found in garbage cans, police files, hotel lobbies, seen in store windows and on the streets and sensed in dreams and horrible accidents.
—Allan Kaprow, "The Legacy of Jackson Pollock" (1958)

Poetry is a revelation in words by means of words.
—Wallace Stevens, *The Necessary Angel* (1951)

We are beginning to see clearly now that in the last decade or so the several categories of the plastic arts have become increasingly indistinguishable. What [now] separates a large drawing from a painting, a construction from a collage or sculpture, and so forth, is not at all easy to define. A kind of interchange is occurring which, besides blurring traditional outlines, is producing a new set of forms that in turn are reconditioning our experience.
—Allan Kaprow, "Some Observations on Contemporary Art" (1960)

This particular strain of experimental literature emphasizes those elements particular to the medium—ostensibly, the resources of language, as applied to sheets of paper or performed before an audience.

When Pound spoke of purifying poetry, he declared, "The Image is the poet's pigment." No, that's wrong. A truer literary analogue from painting's pigment is *words.*

The literary miscegenators, by contrast, emphasize the incorporation of visual and/or aural elements; they appropriate formal ideas developed in the other arts. The collage techniques of Ezra Pound's *The Cantos* echoed earlier inventions in painting, the acoherence of John Ashbery's early poetry acknowledges musical atonality, some of Clark Coolidge's poems echo the choreographer Merce Cunningham's unusual sense of esthetic space, while William Burroughs in 1953 discovered the possibilities of fragmented narrative from listening to an audio collage. While certain contemporary avant-garde writers try harder than their predecessors to echo, if not emulate, the condition of nonobjective painting or abstract music, others have transcended the rectangular page entirely to cast their words in other presentational formats, such as statuary or recording tape or holograms, creating such literary intermedia as visual poetry, sound poetry and holopoetry. Into the tradi-

THE STORY OF ESAW WOOD

Esaw Wood sawed wood.

Esaw Wood *would* saw wood!

All the wood Esaw Wood saw Esaw Wood would saw. In other words, all the wood Esaw saw to saw Esaw sought to saw.

Oh, the wood Wood would saw! And oh, the wood-saw with which Wood would saw wood.

But one day Wood's wood-saw would saw no wood, and thus the wood Wood sawed was not the wood Wood would saw if Wood's wood-saw would saw wood.

Now, Wood would saw wood with a wood-saw that wouldn't saw wood, so Esaw sought a saw that would saw would.

One day Esaw saw a saw saw wood as no other wood-saw Wood saw would saw wood.

In fact, of all the wood-saws Wood ever saw saw wood Wood never saw a wood-saw that would saw wood as the wood-saw Wood saw saw wood would saw wood, and I never saw a wood-saw that would saw as the wood-saw Wood saw saw until I saw Esaw Wood saw wood with the wood-saw Wood saw saw wood.

Now Wood saws wood with the wood-saw Wood saw saw wood.

Oh, the wood the wood-saw Wood saw would saw!

Oh, the wood Wood's woodshed would shed when Wood would saw wood with the wood-saw Wood saw saw wood!

Finally, no man may ever know how much wood the wood-saw Wood saw would saw, if the wood-saw Wood saw would saw all the wood the wood-saw Wood saw would saw.

—Anonymous

tions of Literature come materials, media, artistic scales, and esthetic ideas that have not been used for language before.

Purification is no less "valid" than miscegenation; each direction seems equally capable of generating unprecedented works of the highest excellence.

RUITER

Stap
Paard
STAP
PAARD
Stap
Paard.
STAPPE   PAARD
STAPPE   PAARD
STAPPE   PAARD
STAPPE PAARD   STAPPE PAARD
STEPPE PAARD   STEPPE PAARD
STEPPE PAARD   STEPPE PAARD
STIPPE PAARD STIPPE PAARD STIPPE PAARD
STIP   PAARD
STIP   PAARD
STIP

WOLK

—Theo Van Doesburg (1883-1931)

"ANTI-ART" AND "NOT ART"

There is no such thing as "formless art," for any human creation that can be characterized in any way—as having one kind of structure, rather than another kind—has a particular, perceptible form. The act of characterization is, in itself, an acknowledgment of the presence of a form. The fact that this form may not be immediately definable in familiar terms does not make this work of art "formless." Not at all. The same Jackson Pollock's paintings that once struck many as devoid of form are now regarded as examples of consistent all-over distribution.

Most innovative art has an unprecedented form that, though it may not be immediately defined, can eventually be characterized in a communicable way. It can be shown to be one thing rather than another thing. Such characterizations are the initial problem in criticism of innovative art.

As a rule, when something looks incomprehensibly different and yet seems intrinsically coherent, even if in initially inexplicable ways, it is likely to be formally innovative. A second rule is that the radicalness of a new style can be measured, informally, by the degree to which "establishment" critics respond to it as "not poetry" or "not literature" or, surer yet, by the extent of their effort to exclude it from the

Artists' suspiciousness concerning art had led not to the abandonment of art but to radical experiments with form. It has produced anti-formal art, a contradiction in terms, but a fruitful contradiction.
—Harold Rosenberg, "Literary Form and Social Hallucination" (1960)

Structure is everywhere, there is no place where it isn't.
—John Cage, *Silence* (1961)

Gertrude Stein's question about prose and poetry might be put to the dance. What is dancing, and if you know what dancing is, what is non-dancing? . . . If a performer walks across a stage and calls it a dance, who is to say it is not a dance?
—Jill Johnston, "Modern Dance," in *The New American Arts* (1965)

Any perceptible object or process, in nature, art, or elsewhere, is potentially an aesthetic object. It becomes actually so in being contemplated aesthetically by someone.
—Thomas Munro, *Form and Style in the Arts* (1970)

[Saul] Steinberg's role automatically disguises itself, and his performance continues to prompt people to ask, 'But is he really an artist?'—the question by which each legitimate avant-garde has been greeted.
—Harold Rosenberg, *Art on the Edge* (1965)

A work of art, then, is any artifact in the presence of which an individual plays a particular social role. Furthermore, a work of art is what the perceiver observes in what has been culturally established as an artistic perceiver's space. Thus Andy Warhol's piles of Brillo boxes are works of art because they are exhibited in an art gallery; the situation defines them as works of art, by eliciting in the observer the art perceiver's role. An

publications, the reviewing media, the anthologies, the classroom, and the rewards. When something accepted by an enthusiastic few is still so vehemently opposed, it must be threatening and, thus, must at least be *good.*

It follows that there is no such thing as "anti-art," which is merely a journalistic term temporarily thrown at new work that is so different that it implicitly repudiates the currently dominant styles. Here the use of the suffix *art* acknowledges a possible esthetic validity that, in practice, hastens the disappearance of the prefix. Even Marcel Duchamp's dogged attempts to produce a definitive anti-art were undermined first by his fellow artists, then by the art public, and finally by the art historians and museum curators. Most radical work of the past few decades was, at one time, called "anti-poetry," "anti-literature," "anti-painting," or anti-whatever by someone who should have known better. What David Gascoyne called "anti-literature," in a term memorialized in J. A. Cruddon's *Dictionary of Literary Terms* (1991), is now known as Surrealist writing. Similarly, there is no such thing as "no content," as even the absence of image or words represents a kind of content, imperceptible though it might be to the unsophisticated.

John Cage's compositions have long been dismissed as "not music," even though they are filled with sounds; and Cage's penchant for aural

assertion that such works are not works of art by an observer actually in such a culturally defined artistic space is itself an admission that they are art. That is, it has occurred to such a perceiver that they are. That he should deny what the situation tells him is so is of no importance. The denial of the high-status term *art* to a work we dislike is too common to be taken seriously. The point is that the question should arise. And that it should arise is itself an answer to the question.
—Morse Peckham, "Art and Disorder" (1966)

Personal taste is no grounds for determining what is, or is not, art.
—Michael Kirby, "The Aesthetics of the Avant-Garde" (1969)

I shall simply record the incidents, doing my utmost to exclude everything extraneous, especially all literary graces. . . . I vowed I would eschew all literary graces, and here at the first sentence I am being seduced by them.
—Fyodor Dostoevsky, *A Raw Youth* (1875).

By definition, a work of art is a product of human skill. Its form is artistic as well as aesthetic (this does not imply that it is necessarily good). The concept of art excludes purely natural objects or events, however beautiful, such as wild flowers growing in their native habitat, unaffected by human skill.
—Thomas Munro, *Form and Style in the Arts* (1970).

disorder (i.e., for thoroughly unpredictable relations) inspires others to deprecate his works as
"formless" and "chaotic," even though the consistent disconnection of *ordered* disorder creates its own distinct form (which is, incidentally, considerably different, perceptually, from
disordered disorder).

As the antagonistic posture has more currency in visual art than elsewhere, some artists
speak of their own work as "anti-form," but in
their works the viewer can nonetheless identify
certain structures which reflect essentially formal decisions.

"Not art" is similarly impossible, if the
object at hand can be regarded apart from utili-
tarian reality; and so is "unart." Indeed, anything
under the sun can be considered "art" if either the
creator or the beholder wishes to do so.

The epithet "not art" often functions as an
excuse for a critic's stupidity—for dismissing
what cannot be immediately understood. Yet this
term is intrinsically self-denying, because it
acknowledges within itself the possibility of
accepting this work of "not art" as *art.* In my own
observation, what is dismissed as "not art" is
not necessarily bad. Much of it is dreadful, to be
sure; but so-called "not art" that is *not* egre-
giously derivative or mundane is often very original and, thus, quite interesting.

—Turkish ghazal or circle ode

Alfred Kinsey once said that, "The only sexual acts that are unnatural are the ones that you cannot do." Gertrude Stein: "Human nature is what any human being will do." John Cage: "I have nothing to say and I am saying it and that is poetry," in part because it cannot be anything else (except perhaps "prose"). All were expressing parallel truths.

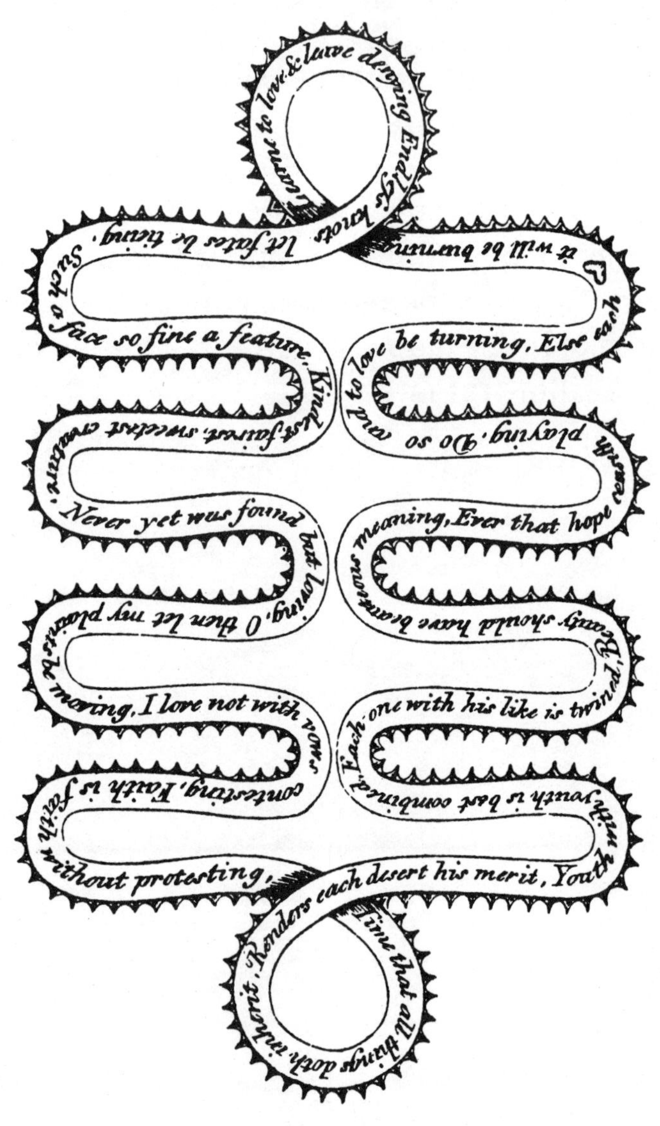

—Anonymous, "Love Knot"

"ART" AS CONVENTION

The term *art* is a convenient convention, because "art" as such does not exist. I use it as a catch-all honorific to define objects and activities that reflect esthetic intention or interpretation; but others use it, perhaps erroneously, to identify an intangible essence that they think may (or may not) exist in the work at hand.

Literature is a sub-category of *art*—reasonable as a descriptive term, but unreasonable as an evaluative epithet (whose opposite would necessarily be "unliterature.")

What exists, in fact, is not "art" but paintings and sculptures—or man-made works that are closer to previous paintings and sculptures than to anything else. Artifacts are the primary medium for art.

Nearly all people I know who are engaged in serious writing regard themselves as making poems and fictions, say, rather than "art." The notion of "making art" strikes us as very quaint—or spurious.

Such person-focused terms as "writer" and "artist" are likewise objectionable, unless they are defined by work, which is to say that a *writer* is only someone who is doing writing, an *artist* is someone who is doing visual art, a *critic* is producing criticism.

In the creative act, the artist moves from intention to realization through a chain of totally subjective reactions. His struggle toward the realization is a series of efforts, pains, satisfactions, refusals, decisions, which also cannot and must not be fully self-consciuous, at least on the esthetic plane.
—Marcel Duchamp, "The Creative Act," in Robert Lebel, *Marcel Duchamp* (1958)

A literary work is pure form. It is neither thing nor material, but a relationship of materials. And, like each relationship, this one too has little to do with length or width or any other dimension. It's the arithmetic significance of its numerator or denominator (i.e., their relationship) that is important. Humorous works, tragic works, world-encompassing or intimate works, confrontations of worlds or of cats and stones—all are equal in the eyes of literature.
—Viktor Shklovsky, "Literature without of Plot: Rozanov" (1921)

The insidious worthlessness of their middling productions subtly corrupts the public deep down in the soul, as is proved by the fact that geniuses usually come into their own only after displacing some pseudo-artist whom contemporaries called great. We must be most conscious of this in painting because we have the word "academic" to denote that appalling competence which so readily outshines true art. But the trick succeeds in every art, until the day when the glamour suddenly pales and the new generation wonders how "taste," "the best taste," could admire such patent emptiness. One answer is: the emptiness helped make the work a playground for familiar feelings; the fraudulent sincerity and skill was the snare which caught both artist and public.
—Jacques Barzun, "Art Against Society" (1951)

When someone who customarily produces visual art writes a book, he becomes a writer, whose work is *writing*, and not an example of "artist's writing" or an "artist's book." Those last two phrases define peculiarities of biography, rather than the nature of the work.

Classifications at their truest define work, not people, who should be free to transcend "a hardening of the categories," to recall Ad Reinhardt's phrase. No *poet* wants to spend his or her entire life condemned to writing just poetry or to have any other artistic activity defined in terms of his or her initial professional designation (e.g., "poet's prose").

An imaginative writer—a true language artist—differs from a "journalist" much as a *chef* differs from a "cook."

AL BUFFET DELLA STAZIONE

—Ardegno Soffici

ALL MATERIALS

Back in 1938, the sculptor Naum Gabo wrote: "In sculpture as well as in technics every material is good and worthy and useful, because every single material has its own esthetic value. In sculpture as well as in technics, the method of working is set by the material itself. There is no limit to the variety of materials suitable for sculpture."

Much the same could be said about working in literature—and often has been said. Only recently, however, have literary artists realized that this liberating assertion includes not only the content of writing but its fundamental materials as well—its paragraphs, its sentences, its syntax, its vocabulary, its paper, and its typography. There is no limit upon the ways in which *these* materials can be deployed.

Why, for instance, should words observe conventional syntax to be considered "poetry" (rather than "nonsense")? Need every line of poetry begin along the left-hand margin, as if lines of poetry had to be aligned like soldiers in an army? The fact that poetry has nearly always been printed that way is clearly *not* an inviolate reason.

John Cage in his preface to *M* (1973): "I now write without syntax and sometimes with it."

Since the small rectangular page need not be the only medium for poetic language, there

We can hope, then, in regard to what constitutes the material and the manner of art, for a liberty of unimaginable opulence. Today the poets are serving their apprenticeship to this encyclopedic library. In the realm of inspiration, their liberty cannot be less than that of a daily newspaper which on a single sheet treats the most diverse matters and ranges over the most distant countries. One wonders why the poet should not have at least an equal freedom, and should be restricted, in an era of the telephone, the wireless, and aviation, to a greater cautiousness in confronting space.
—Guillaume Apollinaire, "The New Spirit and the Poets" (1918)

It seems to me that one can create verse from numbers. The number is a double-edged sword, extremely concrete and extremely abstract, arbitrary and fatally exact, logical and meaningless, limited and infinite.
—Roman Jakobson, in a letter (1914)

Since no form is intrinsically superior to another, the artist may use any form, from an expression of words (written or spoken) to physical reality, equally.
—Sol LeWitt, "Sentences on Conceptual Art" (1969)

What survives of a great artist's work . . . is that part of it which has the greatest density. An artist's supreme work is often assumed to be one in which he has employed all the means at his command.
—André Malraux, *The Imaginary Museum* (1953)

should be no limits upon the media incorporating literature's words—films, videotape, audiotape, photographic paper, holography, plastics and even architecture are all available for heightened language. Just as many materials can be incorporated into language, so language can be incorporated into any medium. If the writer adapts his literary creations to the indigenous possibilities of these "nonliterary" media, one should scarcely be surprised if qualities intrinsic to them affect his use of language. A word embedded in sculpture is considerably different from the same word read in 12-point type on a printed page or, for a second contrast, the same word heard on audiotape. As uncommon language is a sign of literature (as distinct from journalism), so alternative media contain their own capabilities for rendering, or enhancing, poetic words.

—Richard Kostelanetz

MECHANICAL INVENTIONS

The history of stylistic innovation in modern literature is a record of mechanical inventions, each of which reflects verbal ingenuity.

The trick in writing comprehensible dialect—in realizing a spoken informal language in print—lies in developing a mechanical consistency not only in spelling and syntax but also in integrating dialectical peculiarities with familiar language. Without mechanisms to produce roughly uniform results, the printed language would be incoherent.

No good writing is purely mechanical, to be sure; for decisions of taste inform every aspect of composition (including the selection of dialect). Nonetheless, a bit of technological ingenuity can inspire stylistic distinction, apart from any craftsmanly talents. For William Faulkner, for instance, the trick was writing unprecedentedly long sentences; for Dos Passos, it was the omission of certain parts of speech. One reason why the invention itself is more important than "how well it is realized" is that the invention usually incorporates the implements conducive to its realization, much as rhyme and meter functioned in post-Renaissance English poetry.

An initial advantage of a mechanical invention is that it becomes, if observed consistently,

Willingness to experiment is not enough, but unwillingness to experiment is mere death.
—Ezra Pound, "Prefatio Aut Cimicium Tumulus" (1933)

The unconscious element behind invention, which comes when least expected—when the wall against which the inventor has been pushing suddenly gives way—has nothing in common with the age-old heritage bequeathed to us by myths and legends. The latter is one of art's ferments; the former, the victory of an obsession. Every invention, whether a Max Ernst picture or the quantum theory, is an *answer*.
—André Malraux, *The Imaginary Museum* (1953)

The use of devices is a deliberate choice by the writer, and these devices embody style—here the Formalists' concern with the prominent, differentiating devices of separate writers, e.g., neologisms (Khlebnikov), making strange (Tolstoi), digressions (Sterne), oxymorons (Rozanov, Mayakovsky), imagery (Bely).
—Viktor Shklovsky, "The Connection Between Devices of *Syuzhet* Construction and General Stylistic Devices" (1919).

[Jackson] Pollock's all-over "drip" paintings of 1947-50 were in their time taken for arbitrary effusions by his fellow-Abstract Expressionists as well as by almost everybody else. These fellow-artists may have basked in avant-gardist rhetoric about total "liberation," and they may have indulged in that kind of rhetoric themselves, but—as I've said—at bottom they believed in, and acted on, painting as a discipline oriented to esthetic values. Because they could discern little or nothing of these in Pollock, they did not consider him to be a "real" painter, a painter who *knew* how to paint, like a de Kooning, a Kline, or a Rothko; they saw him, rather, as a freakish

a constraint that forbids conventional exposition.

It was a genuinely mechanical trick for Gertrude Stein to scramble the structure of her sentences, or for Hemingway to eschew adjectives and adverbs whose presence could be assumed (his style reflecting the elliptical language of telegrams). One of E. E. Cummings' inventions was the use of one part of speech to function in lieu of another. In places where nouns would normally be used, Cummings put verbs, adjectives, adverbs, and even conjunctions.

> he sang his didn't he danced his did
> what is a much of a which of a wind

> my father moved through dooms of live
> through sames of am through haves of give

In writing *Finnegans Wake*, James Joyce invented a style composed of many tongues, filled with freshly made-up words which, like all neologisms, are essentially mechanical inventions in language. Anthony Burgess, working on more modest levels, fluently incorporated Russian words into otherwise familiar English sentences in his novel, *A Clockwork Orange* (1962). The headlong style of Jack Kerouac's *On the Road* reflects the format of the original manuscript—a single, under-punctuated paragraph that he

apparition that might signify something in terms of cultural drama but hardly anything in those of art proper.
—Clement Greenberg, "Counter-Avant-Garde" (1971)

The page itself can become a material, a statement, the information, the text, progessing or diminishing from page to page. The writer, thus becoming the layout artist of his book, will no longer write stories (or moments) but books.
—Jean-François Bory, *Once Again* (1968)

To understand a sentence means to understand a language. To understand a language means to be a master of a technique.
—Ludwig Wittgenstein, *Philosophical Investigations* (1963)

My ambition is to put everything into one sentence—not only the present but the whole past on which it depends and which keeps overtaking the present, second by second.
—William Faulkner, quoted in *The Faulkner-Cowley File* (1966)

What saves art is invention. There is no creation except where there is invention. Every art has its inventions. The idea of a flat or a sharp in an unexpected place is an invention. A new image (and how rare that is!) can be an invention. An unexpected color put in its place. A new proportion is the composition of a work.
—Max Jacob, "Advice to a Young Poet" (1945)

The sadness is that Kerouac's *On The Road* was never published in its most exciting form—its original discovery—but hacked and punctuated and broken—the rhythms and swing of it broken—by presumptuous literary critics in publishing houses. The original mad version is greater than the published version, the manuscript still exists and some day when everybody's dead will be published as it is.
—Allen Ginsberg, quoted in John Tytell, *Naked Angels* (1976)

typed on rolls of teletype paper. (Only later was it paragraphed, punctuated, and paginated into its presently available form.) All of these essentially mechanical devices produced, among other effects, a heightening of prose and an increase in suggestiveness.

Some writers and critics resist the notion that mere mechanical inventions can change an artist's style, but they fail to perceive that written language itself is essentially a technology of human communication. And like other technologies, written language is susceptible to inventive modifications.

Structural inventions are often dismissed as "gimmicks," but it is precisely such mechanisms that generate innovative forms and styles. The development of a good gimmick can change an artist's career; it can produce flowers in what was previously perceived to be a desert. A new concept, if radically pursued, can draw out of an artist certain capacities for innovation and intelligence that not even he knew he possessed.

The history of modern music is filled with gimmicks, such as the profusion of nonsynchronous indigenous tunes in Charles Ives's best-known music, or Andrés Segovia's transcribing Bach's violin partitas for the guitar, or John Cage's prepared piano, which became a convenient means for avoiding familiar pitches. Glenn Gould's peculiarly hunched-over way of

[Charles] Ives was a thoroughly trained musician; but more than that, he was a great inventor—the equal, in his own field, of Thomas Alva Edison or Samuel F. B. Morse—with several major musical patents to his name. Ives was the first modern composer who consistently did not resolve his dissonances. Instead of returning a piece to its tonic home base, he would end it, metaphorically, out in the field or, sometimes, as in the decisive dissonance concluding the Second Symphony, well into the grandstand. While still in his teens, Ives developed his own system of polytonality—the technique of writing for two or more different keys simultaneously—and in a piece composed at the age of 20 (*Song for Harvest Season*) he assigned four different keys to four instruments. In the *Concord Sonata* (composed 1909-15), Ives invented the tone cluster—where the pianist uses either his forearm or a block of wood to sound simultaneously whole groups, if not octaves, of notes. Another Ives innovation was the esthetics of pop art; for Ives, like Claes Oldenburg and Robert Rauschenberg after him, drew quotations from mundane culture—hymn tunes, patriotic ditties, etc.—and stitched them into his artistic fabric. Other composers had incorporated "found" sounds prior to Ives, but he was probably the first to allow a quotation to stand out dissonantly from the text—all but waving a flag to draw attention to itself—as well as the first, like the pop artists after him, to distort a popular quotation into a comic semblance of the original. Other Ivesian musical innovations include polyrhythms—where various sections of the orchestra play in wholly different meters, often under the batons of separate conductors, all to create multiple cross rhythms of great intricacy. As one of the first modern composers to develop distinctly eccentric musical notations, Ives anticipated contemporary practices of graphs, charts, abstract patterns—manuscripts that resemble everything but traditional musical scores. He also wrote notes that he knew could not be executed, such as a 1/1024 note in the *Concord*, followed by the advice, "Play as fast as you can."
—Richard Kostelanetz, *On Innovative Musicians* (1989)

physically approaching his piano was once dismissed as a gimmick, and what initially seemed a gimmicky way of applying painting to canvas produced Jackson Pollock's mature style.

In literature, many stylistic innovations and idiosyncracies are indebted to syntactical gimmicks. Elements of literary craftsmanship no doubt contributed to the final product; but without the good gimmick, there would be neither an innovation nor a distinctly individual style. For Apollinaire, one crucial trick (indebted to Mallarmé) was merely the elimination of punctuation, which drastically changed the style and flow of his poetry; Faulkner's tricks, besides his penchant for exceedingly long sentences, included the use of several first-person narrators. In drafting both poetry and prose, Ezra Pound always put two spaces between typewritten words, duplicating with technology a characteristic of his handwriting. Words physically separated from one another are perceived differently.

In *Exercises de style* (1947), Raymond Queneau describes the same essentially trivial story in ninety-nine different ways—in various styles, from various approaches—in sum implying that each approach, each style, creates its own credible interpretation of reality. For Julio Cortazar, in his *Rayuela* (1963, translated as *Hopscotch*, 1966), the gimmick was his proposing

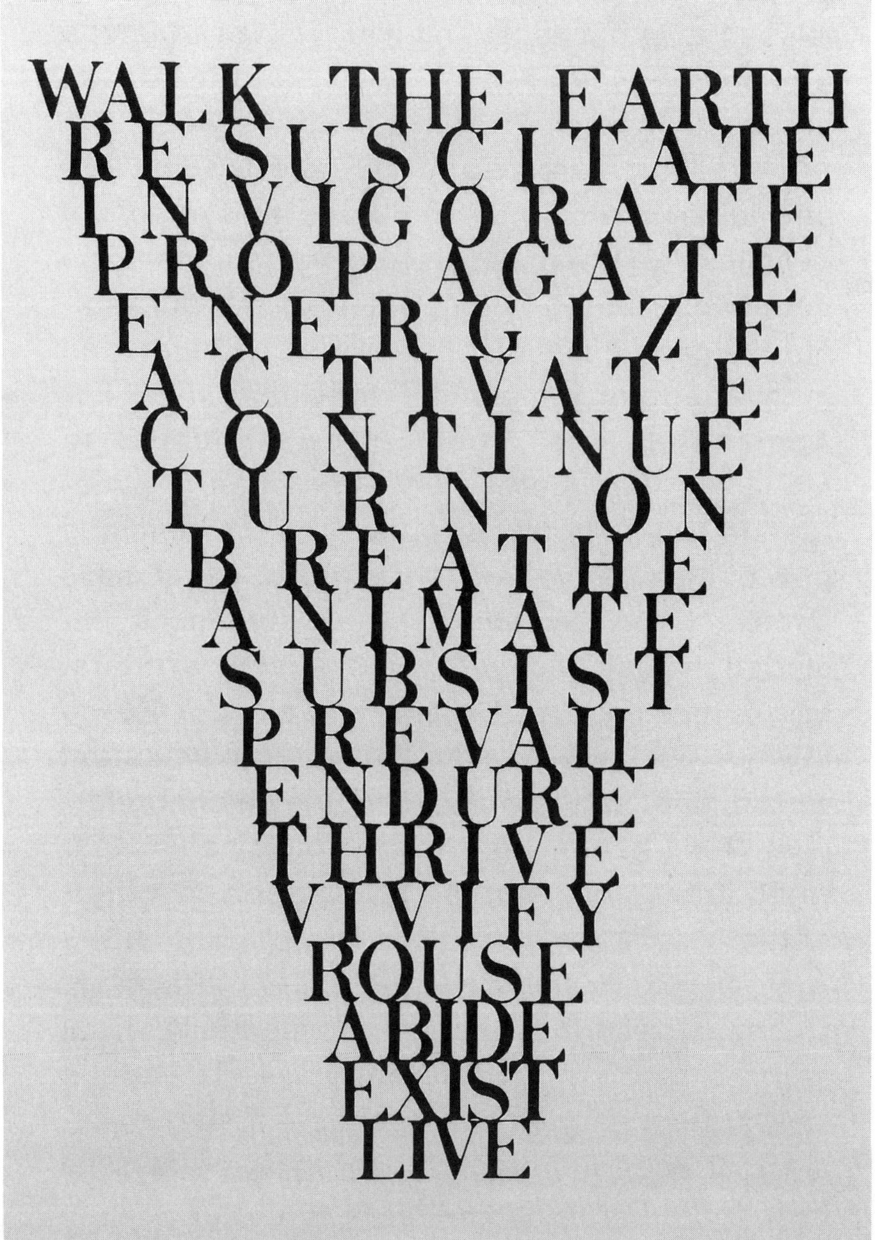

—Richard Kostelanetz

two entirely different ways to read the chapters of his text—either in numerical sequence or by a route that involved skipping around. The point of his gimmick is that merely shifting the order of the chapters can produce a different novel. "This book," he suggests in his preface, "consists of many books, but two books above all." Tom Wolfe, in his preface to *The New Journalism* (1974): "I found that things like exclamation points, italics, abrupt shifts (dashes), syncopations (dots) helped give the illusion not only of a person talking but of a person thinking."

A fertile class of gimmicks in recent art has been the use of nonartistic models, as either content or form; for examples, paintings with popular iconography ("pop art"), a novel written in the form of encyclopedia notations (Richard Horn's *Encyclopedia* [1969]), poetry whose organization is permutational, rather than syntactical; so that methods derived from nonartistic material become both a constraint and a source of irony.

Quite simply, the history of innovative writing is in part a record of good gimmicks.

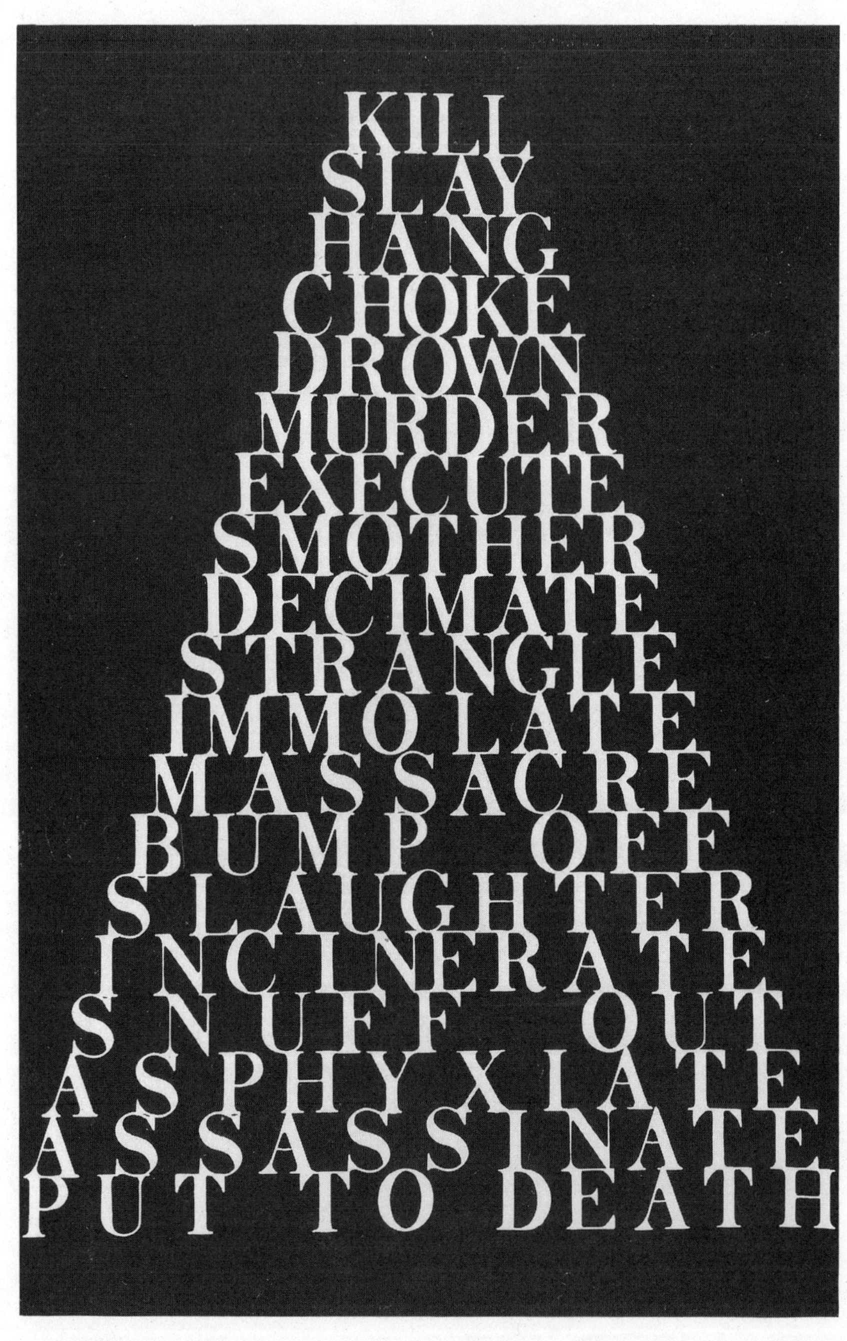

—Richard Kostelanetz

FINNEGANS WAKE

One reason why *Finnegans Wake* (1939) remains a monumental masterpiece is that its particular inventions have never been exceeded. Joyce's book also realized, to an extraordinary degree, certain prime values of literary modernism. One sure index of its excellence is that no other major modern work, except perhaps Gertrude Stein's *Geography and Plays* (1922), is still as widely unread and persistently misunderstood, decades after its initial publication.

Unlike journalism, which tries to render complex experience in the simplest possible form, the *Wake* tells a simple story in an exceedingly complex form. Its subject is familial conflict—among two brothers, a sister, and their two parents. Exploiting the techniques of literary symbolism, Joyce portrays numerous conflicts taking the same familial forms. The metaphors for the two brothers include competing writers, such as Lawrence Sterne and Jonathan Swift, or Alexander Pope and Swift, or competing countries, such as Britain and America, among other antagonistic pairs of roughly equal age and/or authority.

This interpretation of human experience hardly ranks as "original" or "profound," but thanks to the techniques of multiple reference, incorporating innumerable examples into a single

Who then is the hero who achieves the quest? It is not Shem, for here as in *Ulysses* the artist is part of the cycle, and Joyce's view of him is detached and ironic. It is not HCE, nor Shaun, nor even Finnegans, who never does wake up even if HCE does. Eventually it dawns on us that it is the *reader* who achieves the quest, the reader who, to the extent that he masters the book of Doublends Jined, is in a position to look down on its rotation, and see its total form as something more than rotation.
—Northrop Frye, "Quest and Cycle in *Finnegans Wake*" (1957)

Here form *is* content, content *is* form. You complain that this stuff is not written in English. It is not written at all. It is not to be read—or rather it is not only to be read. It is to be looked at and listened to. His writing is not *about* something; *it is that something itself.*
—Samuel Beckett, "Dante . . . Bruno . Vico . . Joyce," *Our Exagmination* (1929)

The book was first published in 1939, though fragments of *Our Exagimination Round His Factification for Incamination of Work in Progress* appeared through the proceding decade. If I dropped the point there I could no doubt leave some readers convinced that I have read *Finnegans Wake*. But I must confess that I have not; I do read in it, from time to time, with great delight until boredom sets in.
—Wayne Booth, *The Rhetoric of Fiction* (1961)

The method is quite simple! You distort the words in a given passage so that they suggest at one and the same time not only the original normal ones but also another series of verbalisms which they now resemble. In order to convey these multiple phrases at once, it is important to respect the intonation of the whole as well as the individual words whose units of sound are being distorted. The procedure is therefore more complicated

text, the theme is extended into an incomparably broad range of experience. Writing in 1929 about the *Wake*, then in progress, Eugene Jolas declared, "The new artist of the word has recognized the autonomy of language and, aware of the twentieth-century current toward universality, attempts to hammer out a verbal vision that destroys time and space." Just as no other piece of writing articulates so many dimensions simultaneously, no other literary work rivals it in textual density.

Congruent with his method, Joyce coins linguistic portmanteaus (where one word incorporates parts of other familiar words), as well as inventing neologisms that echo various familiar words; and the use of many languages serves to increase the range of multiplicity and allusion. He favors puns like "cropse," "tung-toyd," and "o foenix culprit," which serve a similar function of incorporating more than one meaning within a single unit—a verbal technique reflecting the theme of history repeating itself many times over. Thus, the book's principal theme is entwined in its method. As Samuel Beckett put it, back in 1929, "Here form *is* content, content *is* form."

One implication of this method is that *Finnegans Wake* need not be read sequentially to be understood. As the demands of his all-encompassing technique forced Joyce to draw upon

than a series of puns or individual words. Moreover, the words heard in overtone must be systematically related and must contribute to a single planned effect.

—Margaret Schlauch, "The Language of James Joyce," *Science and Society* (1939)

In analyzing these "puns" of multiple meaning, one may come *near* to the author's possible interpretation. But it is the reader's knowledge and education which is the measure of the exact or hit-of-miss explanation. Here are a few samples:

There's the Belle for Sexaloitez!

The multitude of possible meanings are at first almost bewildering, but attempts at a solution are soon transformed into an intellectual game, which slowly becomes a part of the subconscious ability to grasp such sentences and composite words without conscious analysis.

The bell is ringing ("laeuten" in German) for the six o'clock mass; but also Belle, the girl, is there to loiter for a "Sechser" (a "dime" in Germany). Or: Belle is there for sexual loitering; or sex exploitation? Also, every third Monday in April, Zürichers celebrate the "Sechselauten," a Beltane feast, by burning the "Bögg," the demon of winter.

—L. Moholy-Nagy, *Vision in Motion* (1947)

With *Finnegans Wake*, as perhaps with his earlier *Ulysses*, Joyce seems to have attempted to write the culminating work embodying the varied aspects of the contemporary novel: symbolism and naturalism, the psychological as well as the sociological approach, the novel of character and the novel of prototypes.

—Bernard Benstock, *Joyce-Again Wake* (1963)

innumerable examples, the narrative generates a wealth of secondary themes, which are susceptible to remarkably profound particular analyses. Marshall McLuhan, for one, has demonstrated how many striking cultural perceptions can be read into (or out of) the *Wake.*

What also distinguishes Joyce's career is the escalation of his art, as each new book was even more extraordinary than its predecessor. One's mind boggles at the notion of what he might have produced had he lived twenty years longer. Indeed, this sense of esthetic awe, if not incredulity, is intrinsic in our appreciation of Joyce's progressive achievement.

The *Wake* is not a dead end, even on its own terms. Hans G. Helms' *Faim' Aniesgwow* (1959), for one, demonstrates another way to do a polylingual novel.

Whether an individual reader "accepts" or "rejects" Joyce's masterpiece is also, in my observation, a fairly reliable symbolic test of his or her sympathy toward subsequent avant-garde literature. (Another similarly useful test is the more deviant writings of Gertrude Stein.)

—Lazlo Moholy-Nagy, from *Vision in Motion* (1947)

UNCONVENTIONAL CONSTRAINTS

The creation of art depends upon the use of constraints that put a dialectical cast upon imagination. Examples of conventional constraints include meter in poetry and syntax in prose, both of which simultaneously inhibit and enhance the author's powers of communication. One of the best ways to make original art, by contrast, is the use of an unconventional constraint. If the rather ordinary sentence you are now reading were written, say, in dialect, the same idea would necessarily be expressed in a different way. If the dialect were unusual, the attentive reader might not even comprehend the initial idea.

It is unconventional to limit a poem to only a few words, as Robert Lax does in *Black & White* (1971), or to abolish syntax in linear expression, as Gertrude Stein does in this opening to "IIIIIIIII" (1922):

INCLINE

Clinch, melody, hurry, spoon, special, dumb, cake, forrester, fine, cane, carpet, incline, spread, gate, light, labor.

It is similarly unconventional to compose a poem entirely of numbers or to tell a story entirely in nonrepresentational images.

A number of contemporary poets have defended rhyme on the ground that it brings up fresh meanings, words or associations you had not thought of before.
—Rosmarie Waldrop, *Against Language?* (1971)

Simplicity of shape does not necessarily equate with simplicity of experience. Unitary forms do not reduce relationships. They order them. If the predominant, hieratic nature of the unitary form functions as a constant, all those particularizing relations of scale, proportion, etc., are not thereby cancelled. Rather they are bound more cohesively and indivisibly together.
—Robert Morris, "Notes on Sculpture" (1966)

Whereas [Raymond Queneau's] 100,000 Billion Poems uses a combinatorial system to extract a maximum of results from a limited amount of material, the algorithm—while still exploiting the potentiality of circular permutations—seeks to subject them to the harsh selectivity of a reductive form. Its aim is not to liberate potentiality but to coerce it.
—Harry Mathews, "Mathews's Algorithm," in *Oulipo: A Primer of Potential Literature* (1986)

I would ravver read *This Side of Paralyzed* by F. Scotch Fitzgerald, or *Is* (¡) by hee-hee cummings, or a transformation by Ezra Penaloosa of the lyrics of Bertran van Boren, or some delicious little art-novel de Lux about letches of the lousure classes by the rich Mr. Joseph Hoggesheimer, with his love for the glamourous souseland and his faiblousse for lavender and old lychee, or some Lesbian bitters by Robinson Jitters, or *For Lancelot Gobbo* by Gobbineau, or I could tates a little Yeast or Prouts!
—Edmund Wilson, *Note-books of Night* (1942)

The practical advantage of such constraints is this: By forcing the writer to work in previously unfamiliar ways, an unusual compositional rule prevents the creation of familiar work. Not even William Faulkner, say, could "write like Faulkner" if his vocabulary were strictly limited to a few words, or if he cast his language exclusively in photographs or in film or in sculpture. Nor could William Butler Yeats "write like Yeats." One thing such a severe constraint will surely do is produce unfamiliar effects.

What makes the work of the best serial composers interesting—from Arnold Schoenberg to Milton Babbitt—is the amount of variation they can realize within a severe constraint.

Most artistic constraints, if scrupulously observed, generate their own particular range of possibilities, precisely because they make certain solutions more feasible than others. Paradoxically, by discouraging the direct expression of personality, they are also conducive to the realization of characteristic work. If the compositional constraint is a personal invention, then the resulting work will probably look and read like nothing else. Innovative ground rules can stretch the sensibilities of both writer and reader.

If language shapes one's perception of the world, it follows that if language is changed, so is thought. If linguistic syntax were abolished,

train.RR. arbor.Cadaver. appropriate.Tradition. morsel.Tough. pix.RR.
egg.Lieu. chemise.Tree. cathay.Ecologue. fame.Hillbilly. hydra.Anger.
comma.Bound. kkk.Loan. cam.Rama. buicks.Tuesday. mm.Agate. kid.-
NAACP. morose.Kau. rr.Trevelyan. arbor.Reel. four.MM. axe.Aegis.
torpor.Video. jung.Kipper. mm.Apple. cain.Talkie. dali.Shot. mare.Icon.
parade.Risqué. gone.Ad. ggg.Auden. terror.Cot. cam.Rama. reign.Code.
francais.Farmer. ciel.Liable. term.Adore. symbol.Possum. mosaic.Kiss. scal-
lop.Peon. purr.Suede. meal.Oat. rr.Avarice. blague.Cinders. kkk.Arp.
pawn.RR. oak.Asian. hàsta.BB. post.Terrier. rr.Every masque is needed.
reckon.Naître. conga.Regret. rr.Oats. nickel.Laodician. disc.Ghost. verb.All.

feed.RR. rêve.Holt. logger.Rhythm. puzzle.TV. grain.Dios. The man on
the train is travelling from 16 to 35 mm. toque.Charta. kkk.Insular. moo.-
Hair. reel.Aegis. ban.Yoyo. rr.Des Moines. horse.Virus. reb.Style. kew.Cue.
ʃ.Use. wise.Verses. ʃ.Elm. mrs.Minerva. magi.KKK. hell.LP. todos.Lieu.
nazi.Green. double.Croessus. i'm.Ago. rr.The man on the train *est arrivé*.
rr.The pilgrims landed at Victoria Station. ciné.Monde. fresco.Bald.
cancerous.Argot. bodyhead.Press. jazz.US. snow.Job. cash.RR. bag.Abe
Atell. geste.Halt. shack.Treatment. left.Turin. jail.Optic. fm.Hoofer. speck.-
Treacle. goose.Steppe. mm.AD. rr.Ott. whores.Concourse. brecht.Tarrier.
ode.Eon. diner.Shore. terre.Minus. light.Foo. disc.George. fact.Totem.
couvousier.Storey. ether.Reel. books.Yehudi. dolcis.Vista. bains.RR. easy.-
Access. rough.Maniac. sachs.KKK. comma.Toss. amp.Hill. bug.RR. ggg.-
Endor. clock.Asian. cat.Hangar. cue.RR. wimple.Torn. smart.Dialogue.
prick.Aries. pigtails.RR. aye.BB. sublime.Hat. amok.Iran. meteor.Allergy.
ʃ.Até. mm.Addison. valor.Asquith. wren.Askance. rêve.Vulva. sire.Accuse.
swiss.Ide. mr.Cynicism. tease.RR. ink.Lash. cage.Atelier. razor.Dental.
travel.Burro. rr.Dialectically, the circle is square. trains.Pyre. kim.Oona.
nun.Ally. parse.Cur. mm.Irk. the messengers photograph words.RR. rr.The
fucking photographers are monkeys. reel.Tripitaka. agon.Again. nerve.I.
abbey.BB. clan.Dixon. troy.Kerr. gnaw.Think. soccer.Crate. ʃ.Ink. bacteria.-
Logical. cave plus rails equals cage.RR. rounds.Epileptic. couple.Bull.
prick.Aries. fine.Hearts. pansy.Division. goal.Lilith. pagan.Nation. wad.-
Knot. period.Dick. pierrot.Icicle. pillar.Stern. bass.RR. fanny.Brawney.
counter.Attract. skeleton.Reels. ʃ.Shit. ici.Cycle. volpone.RAF. ʃ.Pace.

ʃ.Nye. cleat.Oral. cello.Feign. mel.Yoyo. rr.Omar. came.Den. mm.Arden.
box.Garden. terra.Stychynine. rr.Mauvais. measure.Bibe. kkk.Rape. thor.-
Axe. ʃ.Nues. fray.Wary. univac.Hearse. jar.Indian. tv.Alley. coup.Gott.
reel.Syntax. joliet.Prose. gall.Axis. shoe.Vous. ten.Dentist. ʃ.Rue. chat.-
Nougouchi. foe.KKK. clio.Pitterpatter. rr.RKO. kitsch.Zen. verst.Idea.
collie.Cipher. tome.Matter. mm.Ince. ad.Maudit. airline.Judge. penury.-
Ghandi. mm.Ewes. reek.Instruct. rr.My resistance is law. bolster.VC.
tulle.Box. cement.Terry. tenor.Monument. symbol.Liason. burro.Crate.
hedy.Onanist. type.Reuters. flow.RR. neva.Netherlands. sis.Time. prose.-
Trait. juste.Aeneas. crinoline.Melée. mak.RR. tass.Bulova. razor.Monde.
the man on the train is travelling from Tuesday to Thursday.RR.
bitter.Sound. childe.Dean. times.Square. fat.RR. dada.Weigh. mrs.AAA.
espére.Tante. solar.Terre. venuta.Asbury. vigil.RR. ʃ.Limb. terror.Cottages.
nuts.I. torah.Adore. infinite.Tense. knows.Bleed. magyar.Scene. progrom.-
Muzak. ghouls.Realm. promise.Acuity. uncle.Tomtom. eye.Rat. ram.Blur.

—Frank Kuenstler, *Lens* (1964)

say, thinking would need to proceed in an alternate way.

If circumstances forced you to write in a language other than your mother tongue, you would probably come to think in different terms.

Why not recognize that the page itself has been as great a limit upon literary creation as syntax and try to create Literature that, as an initial constraint, has not just no syntax but no pages.

A truly experimental writer works not with just one constraint but with several.

DIVSAPEXCARNEEFFIGIANSGENETALIALIMI
VITALITERRAECONPINGITSANGVINEGLVTEN
LVCIFERAXAVRASANIMANTESAFFLVITILLIC
CONDITVRENIXANSADAMFACTORISADINSTAR
EXILVITPROTOPLASMASOLORESNOBILISVSV
DIVESINARBITRIORADIANTILVMINEDEHINC
EXMEMBRISADAEVASFITTVMVIRGINISEVVAE
CARNECREATAVIRIDEHINCCOPVLATVREIDEM
VTPARADYSSIACOBENELAETARETVRINHORTO
SEDDESEDEPIAPEPVLITTEMERABILEGVTTVR
SERPENTISSVASVPOMISVCOATRAPROPINANS
INSATIATRICIMORTIFAMESACCIDITILLINC
GAVISVRVSOBHOCCAELIFLVISARCELOCATOR
NASCIPRONOBISMISERARISETVLCERECLAVI
INCRVCECONFIGITALIMALAGMATEINVNCTIS
VNASALVSNOBISLIGNOAGNISANGVINEVENIT
IVCVNDASPECIESINTEPIABRACCHIACRISTI
AFFIXASTETERVNTETPALMABEABILISINHAC
CARACAROPOENASINMITESSVSTVLITHAVSTV
ARBORSVAVISAGRITECVMNOVAVITAPARATVR
ELECTAVTVISVSICECRVCISORDINEPVLCHRA
LVMENSPESSCVTVMGERERISLIVORISABICTV
INMORTALEDECVSNECEIVSTILAETAPARASTI
VNAOMNEMVITAMSICCRVXTVACAVSARIGAVIT
IMBRECRVENTAPIOVELISDASNAVITAPORTVM
TRISTIASVMMERSOMVNDASTIVVLNERACLAVO
ARBORDVLCISAGRIRORANSECORTICENECTAR
RAMISDECVIVSVITALIACRISMATAFRAGRANT
EXCELLENSCVLTVDIVAORTVFVLGIDAFRVCTV
DELICIOSACIBOETPERPOMASVAVISINVMBRA
ENREGISMAGNIGEMMANTEMETNOBILESIGNVM
MVRVSETARMAVIRISVIRTVSLVXARAPRECATV
PANDEBENIGNAVIAMVIVAXETFERTILFLVMEN
TVMMEMORADFEROPEMNOBISEGERMINEDAVID
INCRVCEREXFIXVSIVDEXCVMPRAEERITORBI

—Venantius Fortunatus (ca. 530-ca. 600), "De Signacula Sanctae Crucis"

One well-known contemporary constraint is the use of chance operations in compositions, not only in music but in the other arts as well. Chance operations are usually used to induce artistic selections by procedures other than premeditation, logic, or habit. A composer might throw dice, say, to determine in which order musical notes will appear, or a painter might toss paint in the air and let it splatter on the canvas. Both Marc Saporta's *Composition No. 1* (1962) and Peter H. Beaman's *Deck of Cards* (1989) come as loose pages of prose whose order can be reshuffled forever. However, it is wrong to say that everything "is left to chance," even in these examples, as the painter chose the color of his pigment, as well as the size of his canvas; the writers their characters and scenes; and the composer preselected his notes. Precisely because aleatory devices customarily function to divorce certain (though not all) decisions from the artist's control, they become an effective means for transcending ingrained compositional habits. However, unlike the constraints mentioned before, randomizing procedures are customarily not perceptible *per se* in the resulting work of art.

"Chance" is not identical with improvisation, which actually defines the absence of con-

Chance, as a plunge into "chaos," was the phenomenon through which the artist could glimpse a universal, a-causal harmony that transcended any humanly conceived notion of chaos or rational order. For Duchamp, chance was the tool by which one could break completely with aesthetic taste, with perceptual habits. Tzara tried to achieve a state of total indeterminacy where all predictable patterns, all logical "development" would have been rendered impossible. Chance was also conceived of as a means by which the work of art could "happen" without the intervention of the artist.
—Harriet Ann Watts, *Chance: A Perspective on Dada* (1980).

The scene was bathed in a sea of sounds that had no distinct relation to one another—an atonal and astructural chaos so continually in flux that one could hear nothing more specific than a few seconds of repetition. Fading in and out through the mix were snatches of harpsichord music that sounded more like Mozart than anything else; this music apparently came from the seven instrumentalists visible on platforms raised above the floor in the center of the Assembly Hall.

The sounds came from fifty-eight amplified channels, each with its own loud-speaker high in the auditorium. Fifty-one channels contain computer-generated music composed in octaves divided at every integer between five and fifty-six tones to the octave (five tones, six, seven, eight, up to fifty-six, except number twelve); and since all these channels were going at once, with each operator of the four assembled tape recorders permitted to adjust their respective volumes, the result was a supremely microtonal chaos in which, as Cage's Illinois colleague Ben Johnston put it, "It was insured that no order can be perceived."
—Richard Kostelanetz, "John Cage's *HPSCHD*" (1969)

I can imagine an antistructural criticism; it would not look for a work's order but for its disorder.
—Roland Barthes, *Roland Barthes* (1976)

straint. Proponents of chance suggest that most artists, when permitted to improvise, select the easiest, most familiar solutions, which is to say clichés. However, this is precisely the fault that rigorously aleatory devices, like other constraints, are designed to prevent.

One sign of contemporary genius is the capacity to invent generative constraints. Although John Cage is customarily considered a prophet of artistic freedom, his real forte has been the creation of not one but several alternative constraints. His compositions in sound and print typically allow free choice in certain respects, while implicitly denying it in others, say by his preselection of available artistic materials. The principal musical constraints of his magisterial *HPSCHD* (1969), for instance, stemmed from Cage's initial decisions to have fifty-one different audiotapes, each containing sounds composed in a different scale with successively five tones to fifty-six tones to an octave (except twelve), and then seven live amplified harpsichords randomly playing music from Mozart to the present. Once these constraining ground rules were established, *HPSCHD* already had a particular character; everything else in the piece, from the *I-Ching*-assisted composition of the taped sounds to the decisions of individual performers, could safely be left to chance. The inevitable result was the purest chaos ever heard.

A MOVIE

Eyes are a surprise
Printzess a dream
Buzz is spelled with z
Fuss is spelled with s
So is business
The UNITED STATES is comical.
Now I want to tell you about the Monroe doctrine. We think very
nicely we think very well of the Monroe doctrine.

American painter painting in French country near railroad track.
Mobilisation locomotive passes with notification for villages.

Where are American tourists to buy my pictures sacre nom d'un
pipe says the american painter.

American painter sits in cafe and contemplates empty pocket
book as taxi cabs file through Paris carrying French soldiers to
battle of the Marne. I guess I'll be a taxi driver here in gay Paree says
the american painter.

Painter sits in studio trying to learn names of streets with help
of Bretonne peasant femme de menage. He becomes taxi driver.
Ordinary street scene in war time Paris.

Being lazy about getting up in the mornings he spends some of his
dark nights in teaching Bretonne femme de menage peasant girl how
to drive the taxi so she can replace him when he wants to sleep.

America comes into the war american painter wants to be
american soldier. Personnel officer interviews him. What have you
been doing, taxiing. You know Paris, Secret Service for you go on
taxiing.

He goes on taxiing and he teaches Bretonne f. m. english so she
can take his place if need be.

One night he reads his paper under the light. Policeman tells him
to move up, don't want to wants to read.

Man comes up wants to go to the station.

Painter has to take him. Gets back, reading again

Another man comes wants to go to the station. Painter takes him.

Comes back to read again. Two american officers come up. Want
to go to the station.

Painter says Tired of the station take you to Berlin if you like.
No station.

Officers say give you a lot if you take us outside town on way
to the south, first big town.

He says alright got to stop at home first to get his coat.

Stops at home calls out to Bretonne f. m. Get busy telegraph to
all your relations, you have them all over, ask have you any
american officers staying forever. Be back to-morrow.

What "chance" has in common with any discipline in art is divorcing the result from oneself. (To Cage, the ideal in theatrical performance, say, is sufficient distance to forbid being personally offended if everyone walked out.)

Back to-morrow. Called up chief secret service. Goes to see him. Money has been disappearing out of quartermaster's department in chunks. You've got a free hand. Find out something.

Goes home. Finds f. m. Bretonne surrounded with telegrams and letters from relatives. Americans everywhere but everywhere. She groans. Funny Americans everywhere but everywhere they all said. Many funny Americans everywhere. Two Americans not so funny here my fifth cousin says, she is helping in the hospital in Avignon. Such a sweet american soldier. So young so tall so tender. Not very badly hurt but will stay a long long time. He has been visited by american officers who live in a villa. Two such nice ladies live there too and they spend and they spend, they buy all the good sweet food in Avignon. "Is that something William Sir," says the Bretonne f. m.

Its snowing but no matter we will get there in the taxi. Take us two days and two nights you inside and me out. Hurry. They start, the funny little taxi goes over the mountains with and without assistance, all tired out he is inside, she driving when they turn down the hill into Avignon. Just then two Americans on motor cycles come on and Bretonne f. m. losing her head grand smash. American painter wakes up burned, he sees the two and says by God and makes believe he is dead. The two are very helpful. A team comes along and takes american painter and all to hospital. Two Americans ride off on motor cycles direction of Nimes and Pont du Gard.

Arrival at hospital, interview with the wounded American who described two american officers who had been like brothers to him, didn't think any officers could be so chummy with a soldier. Took me out treated me, cigarettes everything fine.

Where have they gone on to, to Nîmes.

Yes Pont du Gard.

American painter in bed in charge of french nursing nun but manages to escape and leave for Pont du Gard in mended taxi. There under the shadow of that imperishable monument of the might and industry of ancient Rome exciting duel. French gendarme american painter, taxi, f. m. Bretonne, two american crooks with motor cycles on which they try to escape over the top of the Pont du Gard, great stunt, they are finally captured. They have been the receivers of the stolen money.

After many other adventures so famous has become the american painter, Bretonne femme de menage and taxi that in the march under the arch at the final triumph of the allies the taxi at the special request of General Pershing brings up the rear of the procession after the tanks, the Bretonne driving and the american painter inside waving the american flag Old Glory and the tricolor

CURTAIN.

—Gertrude Stein, from *Operas and Plays* (1932)

INTELLIGENCE OF FORM

Embedded in structure itself is an intelligence that exists apart from the writer. A sloppily organized essay will appear stupid, notwithstanding the innate intelligence of its author, while a well-articulated exposition, with every part in its most propitious place, will be taken as evidence of authorial intelligence. Quite simply, someone who can effectively organize a series of English words, whether in print or in speech, appears smarter than someone who cannot.

Form in this sense includes not only the organization of individual sentences and paragraphs but, as well, the larger structures that inform the composition of the whole. These forms not only organize the representation of experience; they also generate imagination and/or intelligence simply by forcing the writer to honor the demands of his chosen structure.

Similarly, mastery of the forms of intelligent appearance, beginning with the language and demeanor of an intellectual, enables a skilled actor to play a person who is measurably more intelligent than he is. Similarly again, we have all met people who, because of their observant imitation of certain manners, initially strike us as far more intelligent than we later discover they actually are.

To be swayed by emotion alone is sentimentality, not art. An
artist who is absorbed not in the contemplation and creation of
forms but rather in his own pleasure or in his enjoyment of
"the joy of grief" becomes a sentimentalist.
—Ernst Cassirer, *An Essay on Man* (1944)

If a man is killed in the street by a car, it is a horrifying
experience to see, but it is not a "tragedy" any more than it is
a novel or an epic. Every writer is constantly on the lookout for
experiences that seem to have a story or poem in them, but the
story or poem is not in them; it is in the writer's grasp of the
literary traditions and his power of assimilating experience to
it.
—Northrop Frye, *Nature and Homer* (1958)

The words of a poem make us remember, in a precise way, what
we already know.
—Christopher Collins, *The Act of Poetry* (1970)

The only new worlds for men are those which the free and
disciplined use of words can help to create.
—Northrop Frye, *The Well-Tempered Critic* (1963)

We thus see the absurdity of that favorite expression of our
traditional criticism: "X has something to say and says it well."
Might we not advance on the contrary that the genuine writer
has nothing to say? He has only a way of speaking. He must create
a world, but starting from nothing, from the dust.
—Alain Robbe-Grillet, "On Several Obsolete Notions" (1957)

The effect of discontinuity is to support that the statements are
existential, and have to be absorbed into the consciousness one

Most writers can speak as well as we write, but we rewrite to sound better than our normal talk. And, in the course of rewriting, we know we are approaching something distinguished when we wonder how the text before our eyes was ever written, for it has become better, far better, than what we normally write or say. This essay that you are now reading was rewritten over a period of two decades to be far denser and more concise than anything I could ever say spontaneously. How it got that way still mystifies (or impresses) me. Because it was rewritten, it was meant to be reread.

A related phenomenon is that certain essayists seem more intelligent in those forms that are familiar to them. Whereas the editorial writer James Reston, say, has been succinct and often brilliant in a few hundred words, he seems prolix and confused in longer forms. If the newspaper column enhances his intelligence, while other forms defeat it, then some of this sense of intelligence should be attributed to the efficacy of the short form in presenting his thoughts; it must embody, at least in his case, a capacity for authorial illusion.

One of the best ways to perceive the intelligence intrinsic in artistic form is to ask why one and only one of a prolific author's many books should seem so much better than the others. For me, the best example of this is Doris Lessing's

at a time, instead of being linked with one another by argument.
Oracular prose writers from Heraclitus to McLuhan have
exploited the sense of extra profundity that comes from leaving
more time and space and less sequential connection at the end of
a sentence.
—Northrop Frye, *The Critical Path* (1971).

It seems a country-headed thing to say—that literature is
language, that stories and places and people in them are merely
made of words as chairs are made of smoothed sticks and
sometimes of cloth or metal tubes. . . . That novels should be
made of words, and merely words, is shocking really. It's as
though you had discovered that your wife were made of rubber:
the bliss of all those years, the fears. . . from sponge.
—William Gass, "The Medium of Fiction" (1971)

The Golden Notebook (1962), which strikes me as
far superior to her earlier fictions (and perhaps
her later novels as well). *The Golden Notebook* is
indubitably more complex, more ambiguous, more
penetrating, more intelligent. The reason for this
superlative quality is surely not its subject—the
experience of an unattached woman—because that
also appears in other Lessing fiction. Nor is the
reason its length, as other Lessing novels are
equally bulky. No, the primary reason for its
superior intelligence must be the form of the four
notebooks, each supposedly representing a different aspect of the narrator, in sum ensuring
that the experience portrayed in the novel is
observed from a multiple perspective. If that
structural concept does indeed generate a complexity of perception—and thus a profundity—that
is absent from Lessing's other work, then it
should be assumed that the formal invention of
the multiple perspective embodies an intelligence that exists apart from the author and,
clearly, thus adds to her own.

A traditional example of formal intelligence in literature is rhyme and meter in poetry,
shaping language with a mind that literally exists apart from the author. In the realization of
an especially pure form is a spiritual resonance.

It is an operational truth that, if an intelligent artist whose head is filled with ideas pays
particular attention to forms, content will none-

ropy gas fibers

unforgettable

glass wrap

Judy

little birthday party

The body is composed 98% of water.

This page contains every word in the book.

—Madeline Gins, *Word Rain* (1969)

theless emerge. Similarly, conventional poets long ago discovered that if they take particular care of sound and structure, sense will probably look after itself.

Most "classic" modern painters progressed from a concern with content to an emphasis upon form.

In beginning a work, the writer chooses not only ends but means (machinery) that will best heighten the available materials and yet bring them to a likely completion. This formal decision assumes the rejection of other available (or conceivable) possibilities.

An esthetic redefinition, if persuasive, can lend intelligence to something that was previously perceived as stupid. For instance, a change in sophisticated perception was necessary before minimalism, in painting as well as sculpture, could be widely considered esthetically acceptable. As Michael Kirby observed, "A person may have little talent for dancing in the traditional sense but become a great dancer by changing the definition and limits of dance."

The essay you are now reading was initially written with each chapter as a single sustained paragraph, and parts of it appeared that way in my introduction to the exhibition catalog *Language & Structure in North America* (1975). Later, I broke the sections apart into smaller paragraphs, each with its own idea, and thus changed the form, the style, and even the content of the work.

STRIPED BASS *(Roccus saxatilis)*, 9 lbs., caught by PETER PONZINI (Aug. 17, 1966) and served that night to his guests for dinner; as TOM JONES was enjoying a second helping, SADIE MASSEY said, "BLACKY FALIS has been coming on to me all summer. I'm going to sleep with him tonight." Tom Jones asked, "Is that why you moved out? So you could sleep around?" Sadie Massey replied, "I am above replying to your vulgarity. If you loved me you wouldn't say things like that." Tom Jones said, "I do love you. The more I love you the more you torment me. I don't think you're wicked. It's the LAW OF DIMINISHING RETURNS." "You overintellectualize everything," said Sadie Massey. Tom Jones came upon a bone in a mouthful of fish. "What an ugly look," exclaimed Sadie Massey. *(See PENNY.)*

TENDERNESS, shown (Aug. 4, 1966) by BLACKY FALIS toward his wife MARJORIE; in the shower in their home, Ptn., Mass.; as Falis soaped up his wife's body he felt a glowing compassion toward her, though he admitted to himself never being in love with her. Actually he thought her vulgar, but strongly admired her independence and vitality. He recalled a period during which his wife had never failed to erotically arouse him by the slightest contact, but this had passed within a few months. He considered that in every way except that in which his present wife experienced orgasm, she was a better mate for him than his first wife, Hildegaard, had been. *(See WATER-SKIING.)*

THC (tetrahydrocannabinol), the active ingredient in marijuana; cited in conversation (July 28, 1966) by TOM JONES in the Cellar Bar in Ptn., Mass. Jones told LAURENCE FAST that research was nearly completed on a synthetic form of marijuana using THC, which could be marketed legally under existing legislation. Fast replied that it was his opinion that the drug could never be legal. "There are too many important people making money off it being illegal, man."

—Richard Horn, *Encyclopedia* (1969)

NEGLECTED DIMENSIONS

One continuing characteristic of experimental art is a concern with dimensions that were neglected in previous works. One typical strategy involves the shifting of emphases and thus of perceptual focus, so that background becomes foreground (and vice versa) or a traditionally secondary concern becomes primary. What the spectator heretofore thought central is suddenly minor or trivial.

If conventional film-making cultivates a moving camera and montage (the editing of film, so that the same subject is perceived from different angles), Andy Warhol's *Empire* (1964), by contrast, emphasizes a stationary camera and the pure continuity of unedited film. It was common knowledge, of course, that the camera could be stationary and that film could have uninterrupted continuity, but no filmmaker prior to Warhol had isolated these options quite so prominently. In music, both John Cage and Earle Brown created works that emphasized silence in place of intentional sounds. If the old literature depended upon syntax and semantics for its principal connections, the new literature depends upon other things; that difference is one measure of its originality.

One reason why a creative artist might choose to neglect certain dimensions is irreme-

I believe in the future of an art which would be the reverse of any ordinary logical or historical method, precisely because our intellects, exhausted by purely rational efforts, will feel the need to refresh themselves with entirely opposite states of mind.
—Charles Henry, "Enquete sur l'evolution litteraire" (1891)

Even the Dadaists by deliberately saying nothing have extended the field of the sayable.
—Rosmarie Waldrop, *Against Language?* (1971)

In 1968, I began to write for the theater which I wanted to see, which was radically different from any style of theater which I had seen. In brief, I imagined a theater which broke down all elements into a kind of atomic structure—and showed these elements of story, action, sound, light, composition, gesture, in terms of the smallest building-block units, the basic cells of perceived experience of both living and art-making.

I want to refocus the attention of the spectator on the intervals, gaps, relations and rhythms which saturate the objects (acts and physical props) which are the "givens" of any particular place. In doing this, I believe the spectator is made available (as I am, hopefully, when writing) to those most desirable energies which secretly connect him (through a kind of resonance) with the foundations of his being.
—Richard Foreman, in *Contemporary Dramatists* (1973)

The concrete movement considered merely as a phenomenon has forced a whole new series of creative confrontations on the use of language, sign, metaphor, typography, and space, and in this there is no going back. While some would disagree that the remarkable designs drawn from the sheer concrete thingness of printers' type and typewriter type . . . have anything to do with poetry, even if they do appear in concrete poetry anthologies, no one surely would fail to accept that a revolt in perception, or

diable personal incompetence. Schoenberg told his pupil Cage that the young composer had no talent for harmony, while Gertrude Stein's college instructors repeatedly criticized her grammatical infelicities. What Cage and Stein share with other artistic inventors is that principle: Ignore your incompetences in order to concentrate upon something else. Cage chose duration in lieu of harmony; Stein invented a succession of alternative grammars.

The following passage from Stein's "IIIIIIIII" is unified not by syntax or semantics but by other qualities indigenous to language—alliteration, assonance, rhyme and rhythm:

> Secret in a season makes the pining wetter. So much hooding, so best to saw into right places the clang and the hush. The held up ocean, the eaten pan that has no cut cake, the same only different clover is the best, is the best.

And this familiar "tongue-twister" emphasizes the musical qualities of language, sound exceeding sense in several ways:

> If a Hottentot taught a Hottentot tot to talk ere the tot could totter, ought that Hottentot tot be taught to say ought or naught or what ought to be taught 'er?

more properly a jolt into perception, has occurred, and that this will increasingly affect publishing, education, art training, and many forms of design, quite apart from the impact on aesthetics itself. There will be no more double-column Spensers with every line turned over because there is 'no space' for it. And perhaps we shall now get Ezra Pound's famous little haiku "In a Station of the Metro" printed as he intended it (and as it rarely is):

> The apparition   of these faces   in the crowd   :
> Petals   on a wet, black   bough   :

Poets have been the slaves of publishers and printers for far too long. They are now beginning to assert themselves.
—Edwin Morgan, "Into the Constellation" (1972)

The external world in which the story's characters live and die is the *world of the author*, an objective world in relation to the characters' consciousness. Everything in it is perceived and depicted within the author's all-embracing and omniscient field of vision.
—Mikhail Bakhtin, *Problems of Dostoevsky's Poetics* (1929)

The vocabulary of criticism will have to include, if it is to come to terms with the meaning of these operations, such words as permutation, conversation, and rotation. It will have to consider the meaning and value of operation such as differentiation, amplification, and reduction.
—William S. Wilson, "Focus, Meter, and Operations in Poetry." *Stony Brook* (1969)

If you drop the idea of imitation as the mainstay of fiction, then the idea that you need "characters" drops away pretty quickly.
—Ronald Sukenick, in an interview (1981)

In his contribution to *The Young American Poets* (1968), Clark Coolidge wrote,"As Stein has most clearly & accurately indicated, words have a universe of qualities other than those of descriptive relation: Hardness, Density, Sound-Shape, Vector-Force, & Degrees of Transparency/Opacity." And Coolidge's own poetry implicitly admonishes readers to pay attention to dimensions of language that they might otherwise ignore.

The apparent elimination of "subject matter" is no total loss for literary art, for language with "nothing to say" is *language looked at*, not through. Poetic devices have intrinsic value, apart from meaning. The French poet Pierre Albert-Birot once suggested that if everything can be said in prose, then poetry should be saved for saying nothing. In my less extreme judgment, poetry should be saved for things that cannot be said in prose, including "nothing."

Such shifting of emphases raises questions about importance in literary art, as well as making us more attentive to artistic dimensions we previously ignored; qualities once imperceptible become perceptible.

This book should probably have an entry on esthetic framing, which is the process of bestowing esthetic significance upon superficially insigificant acts—displaying a urinal as a sculpture, staging four minutes and thirty-three sec-

Le véritable écrivain n'a rien à dire, il a seulement une manière de le dire.
[The true writer has nothing to say. What counts is the way he says it.]
—Alain Robbe-Grillet, *For a New Novel* (1963

Even those paintings that are claimed not to say anything say something by not saying anything.
—Barnett Newman, in a symposium (1966)

Carnivalization is not an external and immobile framework which is applied to a ready-made content, but rather an unusually flexible form of artistic vision, a heuristic principle which makes possible the discovery of new and as yet unseen things. By relativizing everything that was externally stable and already formed, carnivalization, with its pathos of change and renewal, permitted Dostoevsky to penetrate into the deepest strata of man and of human relationships.
—Mikhail Bakhtin, *Problems of Dostoevsky's Poetics* (1929)

Wordlessly but in sounds, that is what the poet is talking about. And it is not in the sounds of music, nor in the sounds that musical notation represents, but in the sounds of speech, in those sounds from which not melodies but words are composed, since we have before us the confessions and the longing of word-creators faced with the making of a verbal product.
—Viktor Shklovsky, "On Poetry and Trans-Sense Language" (1916)

onds of no-sound (and thus miscellaneous noise) in a concert of modern music, fabricating an *Arabian Nights* tale that cannot be found in the original. As Paul Mann puts it, "Duchamp's ready-made was meant above all to frame framing itself." Another kind of literary framing is the blank book (of which I've done two, *Tabula Rasa* [1978], which is a novel; and *Inexistences* [1978], a collection of stories). John Robert Colombo frames conceptual literary criticism when he writes of "Asinius Pollo, the ancient Greek Author of whose work nothing may be said, because not a single line of it has survived."

Der Rabe Ralf

Der Rabe Ralf
  will will hu hu
dem niemand half
  still still du du
half sich allein
am Rabenstein
  will will still still
    hu hu

Die Nebelfrau
  will will hu hu
nimmts nicht genau
  still still du du
sie sagt nimm nimm
's ist nicht so schlimm
  will will still still
    hu hu

Doch als ein Jahr
  will will hu hu
vergangen war
  still still du du
da lag im Rot
der Rabe tot
  will will still still
    du du

—Christian Morgenstern (1905)

---

from X-ing a Paragrab

Sx hx, Jxhn! hxw nxw? Txld yxu sx, yxu knxw. Dxn't crxw, anxther time, befxre yxu're xut xf the wxxds! Dxes yxur mxther *knxw* yxu're xut? Xh, nx, nx!—sx gx hxme at xnce, nxw, Jxhn, tx yxur xdixus xld wxxds xf Cxncxrd! Gx hxme tx yxur wxxds, xld xwl,— gx! Yxu wxn't? Xh, pxh, pxh, Jxhn, dxn't dx sx! Yxu've *gxt* tx gx, yxu knxw! Sx gx at xnce, and dxn't gx slxw; fxr nxbxdy xwns yxu here, yxu knxw. Xh, Jxhn, Jxhn, if yxu *dxn't* gx yxu're nxt *hxmx—* nx! Yxu're xnly a fxwl, an xwl; a cxw, a sxw; a dxll, a pxll; a pxxr xld gxxd-fxr-nxthing-tx-nxbxdy, lxg, dxg, hxg, or frxg, cxme xut xf a Cxncxrd bxg. Cxxl, nxw—cxxl! *Dx* be cxxl, yxu fxxl! Nxne xf yxur crxwing, xld cxck! Dxn't frxwn sx-dxn't! Dxn't hxllx, nxr hxwl, nxr grxwl, nxr bxw-wxw-wxw! Gxxd Lxrd, Jxhn, hxw yxu *dx* lxxk! Txld yxu sx, yxu knxw—but stxp rxlling yxur gxxse xf an xld pxll abxut sx, and gx and drxwn yxur sxrrxws in a bxwl!

—Edgar Allan Poe

MEDIUMISTIC INTEGRITY

One ideal of modernism that frequently gets forgotten nowadays is mediumistic integrity. According to this principle, painting should emphasize effects that are indigenous to the medium of two-dimensional painted canvas, just as sculptures should emphasize their three-dimensionality. A poem should emphasize techniques and purposes that are strictly poetic, while abjuring what is prosaic and fictional. Once the photographic camera had been perfected, what painting gained by avoiding representational verisimilitude was mediumistic integrity—painters painting what could only be painted.

If the reader of a fresh novel can see a potential movie between its lines, then the book he is reading is not a work of fiction but a *de facto* filmscript.

One reason why form is "pure" is that it is noncommercial. Nearly all publishers buy content over form. As a congruence of form and content is desired, the achievement of "absurd theater," say, is discovering ridiculous forms for portraying philosophical absurdity. It follows that anarchist art that isn't counter-hierarchical and open in form has already "sold out."

The indigenous materials of live theater are light, space, movement, and sound (which includes words); so that any live performance

Fixed connections being abolished, the word is left only with a vertical project; it is like a monolith, or a pillar which plunges into a totality of meanings, reflexes and recollections; it is a sign which stands. The poetic word is here an act without immediate past, without environment, and which holds forth only the dense shadow of reflexes from all sources which are associated with it. . . .

It therefore achieves a state which is possible only in the dictionary or in poetry—places where the noun can live without its articles—and is reduced to a sort of zero degree, pregnant with all past and future specifications.
—Roland Barthes, *Writing Zero Degree* (1953)

The proper role of language is only to be concerned with itself—and it is this that nobody realizes. . . . If only it were possible to make people understand that language is like mathematical formulae! These in themselves constitute a whole world; they act only upon themselves; they express nothing but their own marvellous nature and it is precisely for this reason that they are so expressive. And it is also why they reflect in themselves the strange interplay between things and things.
—Novalis.

The less the artist aims at illusionist realism, the more clearly emerges his ideal schema.
—André Malraux, *The Imaginary Museum* (1953)

My first proposition is that the style of a poem and the poem itself are one.
—Wallace Stevens, "Two or Three Ideas" (1951)

that does not exploit all those dimensions is needlessly limited. The essential material of literature is language. The German poet-critic Helmut Heissenbüttel finds in the longer poems of Ezra Pound and Charles Olson "a world of language and nothing but language," but that epithet is even more appropriate for certain prose works by Gertrude Stein, William Faulkner, and James Joyce.

Even though foreign boundaries are approached, experimental work nonetheless initially echoes its original genre. What is called "sound poetry" is primarily poetry, rather than music, and "visual poetry" is similarly closer to poetry than to graphic design.

Marcel Duchamp learned mathematics to make not science but art. Words have status and meaning initially as denotative signs. This cannot be denied or erased. Once divorced from syntax and semantics, language is cleansed and reborn, for unprecedented creative purposes.

If you think it easy to write counter-syntactical language that is nonethless coherent in other dimensions, try it some time. Raymond Federman: "Nothing is more poetic than non-sense." It is *pure* because it is not "about" anything except itself.

Another piece I read at the Six Gallery was simply titled *Poem.*
There was no further title because it was as far as I had been able
to go in poetry.
—Michael McClure, *Scratching the Beat Surface* (1982)

—W. Bleim Kern, "Sound Poetry"

SOUND POETRY

Sound poetry must be heard to be "read," much as visual poetry must be seen. Second-hand descriptions are inadequate. Poetry is *sound* poetry when aural qualities are the principal means of coherence and enhancement, syntax and semantics becoming secondary.

Some sound poetry resonates familiar words; another strain, which might be called *asensical*, creates experiences comparable to hearing poetry in a foreign language. Here the sound poem is successful to the degree to which it invents a language that is "foreign" and yet coherent to everyone:

'Twas brillig, and the slithy toves
Did gyre and gimble in the wave:
All mimsy were the borogoves,
And the mome raths outgrabe.
—Lewis Carroll, "Jabberwocky" (1855)

While that example approximates the *syntax* of a familiar language, other sound poems are, in origins, utopian:

Kroklokwafzi ? Semememi !
Seiokrontro—prafriplo
Bifzi, bafzi ; hulalemi :
quasti basti bo . . .

The only possible solution seemed to be a return to the elements of poetry, to noise and articulated sound which are fundamental to all languages. Schwitters realized the prophecy of Rimbaud, inventing words "accessible to all five senses." His "Ursonata" (1924)—*Primordial Sonata*—is a poem of thirty-five minutes duration, containing four movements, a prelude, and a cadenza in the fourth movement. The words used do not exist, rather than might exist in any language; they have no logical only an emotional context; they affect the ear with their phonetic vibrations like music.
—L. Moholy-Nagy, *Vision in Motion* (1947)

The language lined with flesh, a text where we can hear a grain of the throat, the patina of consonants, the voluptuousness of vowels, a whole carnal stereophony. . . . It granulates, it crackles, it caresses, it grates, it cuts, it comes.
—Roland Barthes, *The Pleasure of the Text* (1976)

I would argue that it is essentially poetry because it isolates facets of words, language in the same way that poetry is a slice, a cutting into experience, a selection of aspects, images, to stand for a larger whole.
—Loris Essary, in a letter (1978)

The relationship between visual poetry and the avant-garde lies in the fact that the avant-garde (from the beginning of the century until the 1960s) has always been "endoliterary": that's to say that it grew out of literature, and that even though it "proceeded" through negations (dialectical negation as the force that produces history), it remains a continuation of the texture of literature, and finally resolved itself into literature once again. On the other hand, visual poetry disrupts the privilege that's accorded to the verbal use of words or to words *tout court*, and it thus places itself outside of literature: it's not

Lala lalu lalu lalu la !
—Christian Morgenstern, "Das Grosse
Lalula" (1905)

One reason why these passages are poetry is that they resemble traditional poetry more than anything else; they clearly are not prose. They cannot be paraphrased.

Some sound poetry is written; other examples are improvised and thus never scored.

a complement to literature, it doesn't make any direct use of the models of literature, it doesn't respect the "genres" of literature, and it finally offers itself as an alternative to literature.
—Eugenio Miccini, "Visual Poetry, the Present, and the Future" (1971)

Among the many untraditional poems John M. Bennett has written, "THE SHIRT THE SHEET" might be the most puzzling, for it consists of nothing but the phrases "the shirt" and "the sheet" repeated over and over—and over and over and over and over. Monotonous? . . . After some initial irritation, I did begin to like it, soon realizing that Bennett was using the sh . . . t form of his two main words primarily as a kind of wind-instrument to do interesting things to vowels with. And so his chant blurred down to timbres, temperatures, sizes, colors, at one point doing nothing but hiss. His sh . . . t form had become a conduit—a chute, if you will—into the elemental myriad-shaped animality that lurks beneath all language.
—Bob Grumman, "Visit to a Minimalistic Poem" (1991)

COMMUNICATION

An artist does not "speak to us" through art; he or she "speaks" only when he addresses his audience directly, "in person." Instead, the artist makes a work of art, and it is this object (not the artist) that "expresses." It says something to an audience, while the artist is off elsewhere, ideally making something else.

As art communicates perception, the role of the artist is the fabrication of something to perceive—not only about its ostensible subject, but about the materials indigenous to art.

The issue in perceptual understanding (as well as criticism) is not "what the artist is trying to do," but what the work is doing, apart from the artist.

Especially in response to innovative work, our original perceptions are often initially inchoate—one knows that one has experienced something new, for that is a feeling embedded in oneself; but it may be a while, a long while, before we discover exactly what.

Our profoundest response to such masterpieces as the *Musical Offering* or the *Grosse Fuge*, say, is the recognition not that this is "the soul of Bach or Beethoven," but that this is the epitome of music; and that perception is what is ultimately communicated.

Poetry is an attempt to make language do more than express; to
make it work; to redistribute intelligence by means of the word.
If it succeeds in this, the problem of communication disappears.
—Laura Riding, *Anarchism Is Not Enough* (1928)

Where the fine arts are concerned, communication is usually of
a fairly complex nature.
—Christopher Finch, *Image as Language* (1969)

The poetry of Dante . . . is a test (a positive text, I do not assert
that it is always valid negatively) that genuine poetry can
communicate before it is understood.
—T. S. Eliot, *Dante* (1929)

So it is with critics—they argue the meaning of art of this or that
but never ask themselves, why should art mean anything? Can
art mean anything? Or the negative—which in this case is an
antinomy: can art mean nothing?
—Dick Higgins, "The Naive and Its Function in Meaning" (1976)

A saint a real saint never does anything a martyr does something
but a really good saint does nothing, and so I wanted to have Four
Saints who did nothing and I wrote the *Four Saints in Three Acts*
and they did nothing and that was everything.
—Gertrude Stein, *Narration* (1935)

The mystery [in great art] comes not from concealment but
from revelation, not from something unknown or unknowable
in the work, but from something unlimited in it.
—Northrop Frye, *Anatomy of Criticism* (1957)

Contemporary literature at its best has clear surfaces; so that the reader can easily discern, at minimum, "what's happening." Writing becomes opaque, by contrast, when its communication is confused, contradictory, unclarified, or incomplete. The reader senses the existence of secrets that the author is withholding. Opacity in art is sometimes confused with "mystery," but the latter term is no excuse for the absence of clarity. "Mystery" in art ideally exists in addition to clarity, not in lieu of it; that epithet is a convenient way of identifying those dimensions of a work that are perceived to exist, but are not immediately understood.

We become mature literary readers when we no longer read for personal advice, affirmation, or gain.

Any perceptible object or process, in nature, art or elsewhere,
is potentially an aesthetic object. It becomes actually so in being
contemplated aesthetically by someone.
—Thomas Munro, *Form and Style in the Arts* (1970)

x g g x g x g x g x g x x g x g x g x g g x x g x g x g x g
x g x x g x g x g x x g x x g x g x g x g x g x g g x g x g
g x g x g x g x x g x g x g x x g x g x x g x g x g x g x g
g x g x g g x g x g x g x g g x g x g x x g x g x g x g g x
g x g x g g x g x g x g g x g x g g x g x g x g x g x x g x
g x x g x g x g x g x g x g x g x x g x g x g x g x g x g x
g x g x g x x g x g x g x g x g x g x x g x g x g x g x g x
g x g x g x g x g x g x x g x g x g x g x g x g x g x g x g
x g x g x g x g x g x g x g x g g x g x x g x x g x g x g x
g x g x x g x g x g x g x g x g x g x g x g x g g x g x g x
g x g x g x g x g x g x g x x g x g x g x g x x g x g x g x
g x g x g x g x g x g x g g x g x x g x g x g x g x g g x g
x g x g x g g x g x g x g x g g x g x g g x g x g x x g x g
x g g x g x g x g x x g g x g x g x g x g x g g x g g x g x
g x g x x g x g g x g x g x g g x g x g x g x g x g x x g x

—José Luis Castillejo, *El Libro de las Dieciocho Letras* (1972)

Criticism and reviewing—the two are not the same. The latter consists of mostly immediate responses to new work; the former term honors considered reflection. Criticism at its best is not designed to curry favor with artists, publishers, producers, or one's teachers. It is meant to discriminate and illuminate. Whereas most reviewing functions as publicity, criticism that echoes common sentiments is just opportunistic self-congratulation. Too many "critical" magazines nowadays resemble symposia about terrorism, which are inevitably boring, because everybody is opposed.

Serious consistent critics can be divided into conservatives and radicals. The former prefer works that formally resemble the milestones of the past; conservatives relish the author's respect for traditional artistic "verities" and the fulfillment of familiar expectations.

Radical critics, by contrast, prefer works that are formally unlike anything they have experienced before. They appreciate not only the disruption of perceptual expectations but also fundamental challenges to their sense of "Art." Since art will change as rapidly as life, they assume that the most relevant new art will be as different from the past as their own experience differs; the most valuable new work will repre-

In essence, there is a kind of intellectual polarization taking place around the mid-twentieth century which separates the intellectual establishment into two—one, those who are still preoccupied with the world as conditioned by its pre-1900 parameters, and those who are attempting to recast and reorient their world view to one which is in many ways quite unprecedented in human experience.
—John McHale, "Toward the Future" (1968)

The best work is always neglected and there is no critic among the older men who has cared to champion the newer names from outside the battle. The established critic will not read. So it is that the present writers must turn interpreters of their own work.
—William Carlos Williams, "Marianne Moore," *The Dial* (1925)

A work of art is perceived against a background of other works of art and in conjunction with them. The form of a work of art is determined by its relation to other forms that preceded it . . . . Not parody alone, but every work of art is created as a parallel and contrast to some sort of model.
—Viktor Shklovsky, *Theory of Prose* (1929)

Whether we like it or not—and many dislike it intensely—there has been a gap between the composer and audience for the past three hundred years. It is a function of musical criticism to close the gap, so far as a structure of words can do so; perhaps it would be better to say that it is the function of musical criticism to speed the closure rather than effect it, for criticism, obviously, cannot take the place of art.
—Alfred Frankenstein, in *The Modern Composer and His World* (1961)

sent an innovative interpretation of a perceptible artistic issue or of an acknowledged tradition.

The recurring major problem for the radical critic is distinguishing genuine artistic advance from temporary fads, some of which mas-
querade as advanced art. What separates the
perspicacious critic from the dunderhead is that
the former's judgments are accepted, if only
echoed, by future artists and audiences.

While the conservative bows before familiar dieties, the radicals tend to feature artists'
names that are either controversial or unknown.
The conservative critic likes epithets such as
"masterpiece," which purportedly connect a new
work to the ages, while the radical prefers more
temporal language. Radicals base their judgments upon a sense of historical change; conservatives, upon historical continuity. Conservative
critics are, by definition, those who continually
object to the emerging avant-gardes.

Radicals are more inclined than conservatives to do their own creative work, to become
cultural middlemen (e.g., agents, anthologists,
curators), and to write polemical critiques of
cultural dissemination—the first, because radical critics tend to be closer than conservatives
to the creative processes of contemporary art;
the second, because their biases make them
aware of first-rate work that needs their help to

It is in the character of the critic to say no more in his best moments than what everyone in the following season repeats; he is the generator of the cliché.
—Leo Steinberg, "Jasper Johns: The First Seven Years of His Art" (1962)

Critics have always been howling about unintelligibility, though if a difficult book has existed long enough, they will not complain too loudly of what they say they cannot fully understand.
—Anthony Burgess, *Rejoyce* (1965)

Is the activity of criticism a departure alone, or does the critic incur a responsibility to restore order?
—Peter H. Barnett, *Can You Tell Me How* (1980)

Perhaps the most potent 'ideology' motivating critics who also happen to be writers of fiction or poetry is the set of literary values implicit in the literature they themselves write. In a 1961 essay T. S. Eliot reflects that "in my earlier criticism, both in my general affirmations about poetry and in writing about authors who had influenced me, I was implicitly defending the sort of poetry that I wrote and my friends wrote. . . . I was in reaction not only against Georgian poetry, but against Georgian criticism; I was writing in a context which the reader of today has either forgotten, or has never experienced."
—Grant Webster, *The Republic of Letters* (1979)

The present crisis in the humanities originated in the postwar English Department, which was and is a parochial construction. The folly was in thinking that you could make critics by training them just in criticism. Criticism without learning is futile. It produces lightweights, poseurs, triflers.
—Camile Paglia, "Junk Bonds and Corporate Raiders" (1991)

enter the cultural marketplace; and the last, because they inevitably wonder why the art they admire is not earning its just rewards.

Criticism is best written in the language of one adult communicating with another. Jargon and other artificial circumlocutions serve not to illuminate but to display its author's privileges, much as fancy clothes or an expensive car might, and thus intimidate readers with the trapping of fashionable appeance. Uncommon lingo serves the social function of announcing that the speaker belongs to a rarefied class; incomprehensibility tied to academic authority is inherently fascist, even when serving purportedly liberal or left-wing sentiment. Obscure writing directed at students resembles formally as well as functionally the barely intelligible commands of a perverse drill sergeant.

A "critic" ignorant of the corruptions implicit in the uneven dissemination of good art has his or her head buried in the sand.

A "critic" lacking a coherent viewpoint is really a "reviewer," who dares not collect his judgments into a book, because his notices, when read together, will reveal improvisational opportunism.

A "critic" unresponsive to innovation in art is ultimately not a *critic* but a *caretaker.*

R   R
    R   R   R
REK   REK
    RAK   RAK   RAK
TREK   TREK
    TRAK   TRAK   TRAK
STREK   STREK
    STRAK   STRAK   STRAK
STREKKEN STREKKEN
STRAK   STRAK   STRAK

STREKKEN

STRAK

—Til Brugman (1888-1958)

When you hear the epithet "critical theory," you know that someone wants you to feel servile.

Truly experimental art incorporates a measure of risk, as well as a capacity to offend. By contrast, any work that is instantly, universally acceptable critically cannot possibly be experimental. This last principle applies additionally to the reception of arts criticism.

The ultimate concern of criticism is our consciousness of art; that is also the ultimate concern of art.

SYMPHONY NO. 3

$$1+2 = 3$$
$$4+5+6 = 7+8$$
$$9+10+11+12 = 13+14+15$$
$$16+17+18+19+20 = 21+22+23+24$$
$$25+26+27+28+29+30 = 31+32+33+34+35$$
$$36+37+38+39+40+41+42 = 43+44+45+46+47+48$$
$$49+50+51+52+53+54+55+56 = 57+58+59+60+61+62+63$$
$$64+65+66+67+68+69+70+71+72 = 73+74+75+76+77+78+79+80$$
$$81+82+83+84+85+86+87+88+89+90 = 91+92+93+94+95+96+97+98+99$$

In the above number symphony note the following facts:

1. The number of terms to the left of the equal sign is always one greater than the number of terms to the right of the equal sign and the product of these will always give you the middle number. Thus, in the first case (1+2 = 3) we had two terms to the left and one on the right and the product of these gives the middle number, 2.4+5+6 = 7+8—three terms times two terms equals 6, which is the middle number. In the next row we have four terms times three terms which is 12, or the middle number.

2. Note that all the first numbers are perfect squares—that is, 1, 4, 9, 16, 25, etc. Note also that the difference between any number and the number directly above it is always the same for each row and progresses by 2. For example: to go down the middle numbers, 2, 6, 12, 20, 30, etc., we have the difference 4, 6, 8, 10, 12, etc. This is true for any of the other numbers, as you can easily verify.

—Royal Heath

AUTHOR AND ART

What the work actually communicates may be quite different from what the artist thinks (or says) he or she intended. In case of disputes, the ultimate source of evidence is not the artist but his or her work. If the painter tells us that his green landscape is "depicting a skyscraper," we consider his advice but ultimately respect his art. Trust not the teller but the tale, because the teller can fib in ways that the tale cannot.

Every work of human imagination no doubt reflects (and reveals) peculiarities of its creator, but what these might be is hard to identify without prior acquaintance with the person. As a rule, if viewers are not personally acquainted with a living artist, they cannot justifiably claim any knowledge of the artist's intentions or his ideas or his mental proclivities. Doing so is not only fallacious but presumptuous.

Similarly, knowing an artist apart from his work is no sure guide to imagining what his art might be.

All human creations, no matter how superficially "impersonal," reflect human decisions; Ortega y Gasset's "dehumanization of art" is really a contradiction in terms, much like "unnatural sex." Ad Reinhardt, whose sense of what he was doing as an artist was remarkably honest, accurate, and profound, testified, "Once [Robert

The external world in which the story's characters live and die
is the *world of the author,* an objective world in relation to the
characters' all-embracing and omniscient field of vision.
—Mikhail Bakhtin, *Problems of Dostoevsky's Poetics* (1929)

We can never forget that what books communicate often remains unknown even to the author himself, that books often say
something different from what they set out to say, that in any
book there is a part that is the author's and a part that is a
collective and anonymous work [or is intrinsic in the book's
material].
—Italo Calvino, *The Uses of Literature* (1986)

I know that their essential being, quite like my own, is outside
what they write and that only the most despicable of one's
contemporaries confuse the value of a man's collected works
with that of his life.
—Leslie A. Fiedler, *No! in Thunder* (1960)

Under no circumstances should the reader infer from my
comments on Rozanov's domesticity that Rozanov was "pouring
out" his soul to the reader. No, he had assumed the "confessional
mode" as a device.
—Viktor Shklovsky, "Literature without a Plot: Rozanov" (1921)

Yet if the only form of tradition, of handing down, consisted in
following the ways of the immediate generation before us in a
blind or timid adherence to its success, "tradition" should
positively be discouraged. It involved, in the first place, the
historical sense, which . . . compels a man to write not merely
with his own generation in his bones, but with a feeling that the
whole of the literature of Europe from Homer and within it the
whole of the literature of his own country has a simultaneous

Motherwell] said of abstract expressionism that the abstract part was the art part and the expressionism was the human part. . . . But that's a disgraceful dichotomy. The abstract part is human by itself. Abstract art is only made by humans. No animals or vegetables make it."

"Inhuman literature," by definition, would have to be something that human beings cannot do.

Style reflects not "the man," as some would have it, but the author's particular talents, which may be as much innate as developed, and then his or her conscious decisions about the materials of articulation.

An innovative style is less personal than characteristic, though stylistic idiosyncracies no doubt reflect personality—much like the furniture in one's house.

A prime deceit of literary politicking is making the writer (and his or her professional associations) more important than what he or she writes. It joins advertising and promotion in manufacturing an appealing persona (even if this myth is drastically different from the author's actual personality). Whenever biography is promoted over art, whether in merchandising a new book or curating an exhibition, say, one implication is a negative opinion of the artistic worth of whatever is being pushed. What, in fact, we see is not an artist but his or her words.

existence and composes a simultaneous order. This historical sense, which is a sense of the timeless and of the temporal together, is what makes a writer traditional. And it is at the same time what makes a writer more acutely conscious of his place in time, of his contemporaneity.
—T. S. Eliot, "Tradition and the Individual Talent" (1919)

Poets lie, both to themselves and to everyone else, about their indebtedness to one another, and most critics and literary scholars tend to follow poets by hopelessly idealizing all inter-poetic relations.
—Harold Bloom, *Figures of Capable Imagination* (1976)

What will vanish is the figure of the author, that personage to whom we persist in attributing functions that do not belong to him, the author as an exhibitor of his own soul in the permanent Exhibition of Souls, the author as the exploiter of sensory and interpretive organs more receptive than the average.
—Italo Calvino, *The Uses of Literature* (1986)

Finally, the author has been the victim of many attacks, ranging from the petty to the downright dangerous, by various vested interests as well as parties in two-piece suits; the nature of some of these assaults is touched upon in the pages that follow, but one of the charges, the vilest, most scurrilously scandalous of them all, must be mentioned here: the insinuation, some-times made subtly and sometimes blatantly, that P. D. Q. Bach is a figmental entity, a being no less the creation of this author than was Tarzan of Edgar Rice Burroughs, or Howard Hughes of Clifford Irving. It should be unnecessary for a tenured univer-sity professor to defend himself against such a patently false accusation, such an absurd calumny, such a big fat lie, but under the circumstances he must welcome the opportunity provided in these pages to present the evidence and, it is hoped,

New art is made not by groups, regardless of how many banners they collectively wave, but by work that is produced by individuals. One difference between Americans and Europeans is our suspicion of coteries and of coterie-promotions for nothing more than a coterie. (And no bitterness can match that of those who fail through excessive vulgarity.)

One assumption of putatively personal poetry is the superior humanity of the poet, but neither reading poetry nor writing it necessarily makes a human being more human. Indeed, every writer knows that the demands of his trade are often deleterious, and rare is the poet who has not at one time in his life been hideously insensitive, for the sake of his art, to the demands of humanity around him. (Poetry readers have no doubt committed similar neglects in the course of appreciating poetry.) The best measure of superior human character is good works in the world, not well-meant, sentimental poetry.

Conversely, the only true definition of "madness" in art is the creation of work or activities that *would not have been done before* (as distinct from "hadn't been done before"). That epithet refers to work that might have been conceived, "thought of," but hadn't been done until the "mad" artist did it, which is to say that he or she did what others did not dare, "madness" being a euphemism for courage, even if the men-

silence forever the seemingly numberless Doubting Thomases, Richards, and Harolds who (to our external shame) fill most of our musical chairs.
P.S.//University of Southern North Dakota at Hoople//23 July 1975//11:47 pm
—Professor Peter Schickele, *The Definitive Biography of P. D. Q. Bach* (1976)

It was play rather than work which enabled man to evolve his higher faculties—everything we mean by the word "culture." . . . Play is freedom, is disinterestedness, and it is only by virtue of disinterested free activity that man has created his cultural values. Perhaps it is this theory of all work and no play that has made the Marxist such a very dull boy.
—Herbert Read, *Anarchy and Order* (1954)

All bad art comes from returning to Life and Nature, and elevating them into ideals.
—Oscar Wilde, *The Decay of Lying* (1889)

tality informing the work was indeed quite sane. *Finnegans Wake* is made in this sense; so is Nabokov's *Pale Fire* (1962) or an underappreciated book which it resembles, Professor Peter Schickele's *The Definitive Biography of P. D. Q. Bach* (1976). This last is an illustrated "life and times" of a fictional figure, written by an indubitably foolish "Professor" whose name is otherwise similar to that of the man who holds the copyright.

Pure madness, of the certifiable, institutional kind, is customarily counter-productive, in art as well as life.

—Man Ray (1924)

GENRES

Here and elsewhere, I have usually regarded the corpus of human writing as divided into the traditional genres of poetry, fiction, drama, and the essay. Genre is the literary equivalent of the biological *genus*—a subordinate class with common distinguishing characteristics.

Although much experimental writing tries to demolish the separating barriers, these terms still strike me as valid and useful. Not only is most writing, even most experimental writing, conceived with reference to particular generic categories—we speak of "experimental fiction" or "visual poetry"—but, indeed, nearly all experimental literature published today clearly belongs to one genre rather than another.

In brief, the common distinguishing characteristics of poetry are personalized expression that favors conciseness and the acknowledgement of forms that can be restrictive to various degrees. "Fiction" favors language that is more freely formed ("prose") to create a less personal world of self-referring activity and thus favors extended narrative. "Drama" consists of scenarios to be realized in performance. "Theater" is sound, light, and movement before a live audience. "Essays" confront particular subjects with a high degree of ideation and explicitness.

For me, as a writer, the poem as opposed to other forms of literature has a number of advantages; it can be clearly defined and sharply contoured; in a small space and with little material, it is able to store a relatively high energy and with this produce a relatively strong impression; compared to other genres, the poems—and among modern ones, particularly the concrete poem—is a very rational product and thus especially suited for modern industrial society, with its various propensities for rationalization.
—Ernst Jandl, in a speech (1968)

The nature of the difference between what is termed prose on the one hand and verse on the other is not to be discovered by a study of the metrical characteristics of the words as they occur in juxtaposition. It is ridiculous to say that verse grades off into prose as the rhythm becomes less and less pronounced, in fact that verse differs from prose in that the meter is more pronounced, that the movement is more impassioned and that rhythmical prose, so called, occupies a middle place between prose and verse.

It is true that verse is likely to be more strongly stressed than what is termed prose, but to say that this is in any way indicative of the difference in nature of the two is surely to make the mistake of arguing from the particular to the general, to the effect that since an object has a certain character that therefore the force which gave it form will always reveal itself in that character.

Yet, quite plainly, there is a very marked difference between the two which may arise in the fact of a separate origin for each, each using similar modes for dis-similate purposes; verse falling most commonly into meter but not always, and prose going forward most often without meter but not always.
—William Carlos Williams, *Spring and All* (1923)

It is true that some new literature tries to blur these distinctions especially when its author takes the motives and techniques of one genre and integrates them with another—for examples, "narrative poetry" and "lyric fiction." Part of the interest in works of this kind is precisely the tension between the demands of particular genres and the artist's propensities for invention. (A similar tension informs pulverizing experiments with sentence structure, with words, and even with diction.)

Nonetheless, no matter how hard an artist tries to balance the demands of one genre against another, the resulting work usually falls into one or another category.

Whereas the medium of poetry is words, the medium of drama
is people moving about on a stage and using words.
—Ezra Pound, *ABC of Reading* (1934)

Flaubert and De Maupassant lifted prose to the rank of a fine art,
and one has no patience with contemporary poets who escape
from all the difficulties of the infinitely difficult art of good
prose by pouring themselves into loose verses.
—Ezra Pound, "Vorticism" (1914)

Essays differ from poetry and fiction in striving for direct engagement with personal experience and worldly realities. Poetry and fiction proceed from interior understanding; essays from exterior knowledge. The subject of an essay is more explicit than implicit, as the essayist never loses sight of his chosen concerns. Essays strive to be true in ways unavailable to fiction or poetry. "Essay" is commonly used as an honorific term to characterize expositions that, for reasons of style, do more than merely expose.

In essays, unlike fictions, the author speaks directly, rather than symbolically or metaphorically; he favors definition and communication over implication and ambiguity. Since an essay tries to communicate an author's understanding, one measure of "success" is the reader's comprehension of the author's thoughts.

Some of the most original contemporary fictions come disguised as essays that implicitly test your sensitivity to fiction—only fools would accept them as wholly true.

Since essays are inspired by experience, rather than by literary precedents, essayistic form should ideally follow function; optimally, the essayist should reinvent a form for every new function. One reason why this opportunity has rarely been taken is that people writing about

	HELL of the Pure Deed — Power without Purpose			← Search for Salvation by finding refuge in Nature	THIS WORLD — Dualism of Experience / Knowledge of Good and Evil / Existential Being	Search for Salvation by finding release from Nature →	HELL of the Pure Word — Knowledge without Power		
The Fall									
Primary Symbol	Sea		Common Night	Forest	City	Mountain	Private Light		Desert
Secondary Symbols	Blood	Tears	Serpents	Wild Beasts	Domestic Pets	Birds	Machines	Insects	Abstract shapes
Myth Symbols	Dragons	Sirens	Hidden Treasure	Dwarves Giants	The Hero The Ring	Witches	Ghosts		The Magician's Castle
Metaphysical Condition	Pure Aesthetic Immediacy Pure Ethical Potentiality			Art	Actualisation of the Possible Growth Soul = Spirit	Science	Aesthetic Nonentity Pure Ethical Actuality		
Order	Monist Unity (water) Barbaric Vagueness			Rivers Country	Differentiated Unity Civilisation	Roads Town	Dissociated Multiplicity Decadent Triviality		
Time	Natural	Cyclical Circle	Reversible Everlasting Change	Historical	Irreversible Process Change Spiral		Static	Eternal Turbine	Unchanging
Relation Between Selves	Mutual Irresponsibility Encroachment			The Vow	Conscious Relations Neighbourliness	The Contract	Mutal Aversion Desertion		
Relation to Self	Self-Sufficiency			Low brow Masses	Self-realisation	High brow Rulers	Self-negation		
Mental Life	Stream of Sensations			Sensation Memory Intuition	Generalized patterns of feeling Important facts	Thinking Logic Feeling	Empty Abstractions		
Requiredness	Objective Instinctive Determined			Venere Vulgare Blind Eros	Subjective Grace Agape	Venere Celeste Seeing Anteros	Conscious lack of requiredness The void of Indecision or Self-Reflection		
Sin	Sensuality			{Criminals Bohemians}	Anxiety	{Police Bourgeois Pharisees}	Pride		
Sex	Incest (The Walsung)			Romantic Adultery (Tristan)	Marriage	Sophisticated Adultery (Figaro)	Promiscuity (Don Giovanni)		
Physical Diseases	Cancer			Digestive-Venereal		Sensory-Respiratory	Paralysis		
Mental Diseases	Idiocy			Epileptics Manic-Depressives		Paranoiacs Schizophrenics	Dementia Praecox		
Religion	Blind Superstition (Animism)			Pantheism	(Cath.) Faith (Prot.)	Deism	Lucid Cynicism (Logical Positivism)		
Theories				Irrational Emotionalism		Rational Legalism			
Art	Dada Art			Surrealism		Cubism	State Art		
Politics	Tyranny (Fascism)			Feudal Aristocracy		Laissez Faire Democracy	Anarchy (Economic Collapse Class War)		
Political Slogans	Fraternity				Justice		Liberty		
Hero	The Tragic Hero–Outlaw with S[ex] A[ppeal] Flying Dutchman Vamp			Marx Bros.	The Comic or Ironic Hero Don Quixote The Beggar Byron's Don Juan The Idiot (Dost.) The Child (Alice) Detectives (Holmes)		The Demonic Villain without natural S[ex] A[ppeal] Iago Stavrogin The Grand Inquisitor Depraved or Cissy Master-Crooks		
The Quest	The Voluntary Journey of the corrupt mind through the Sea. Purgation of pride by Dissolution			Fertilising the Waste Land The Island	PURGATORY Forgiveness	Draining the Swamp The Oasis	The Voluntary Journey of the corrupt body through the Desert Purgation of Lust by Dessication		

PARADISE
(The City of God)

—W. H. Auden

their own understandings nearly always observe conventional structures, rarely considering how else their subjects might be approached. The question to ask, each time an essay is written, is what form would be more appropriate for communicating the author's sense of this particular experience.

A detailed chart is an essay; so is the front page of a newspaper (its subject being major events of the day before). Both of them offer disconnected details that need to be read consecutively. Thus, these essays are designed to be "dipped into" and perused; they cannot be read from "beginning to end," simply because they have neither beginning nor end.

The essay you are now reading was written differently from most of my expository writing, which tends to be more introductory than theoretical, in part because this essay has something radically different to say and is thus designed to have an impact different from most of my prose.

Though most literary criticism appears in essay form, the critical literature on essaying is remarkably slight; that on innovative and alternative literary exposition, almost nonexistent.

If it has been said that many of Krucenyx's most famous avant-garde works are "a unique combination of the hieratic and the throwaway," the autographic series may well be seen as closer to a pure "throwaway." One fears that if such a booklet were to come into the hands of an uninitiated person, it might literally be thrown away as a juvenile doodling of no value. Perhaps some works in the series have in fact totally disappeared for exactly this reason. Their appearance is certainly humble and unprepossessing, unlikely to be recognized as even books, much less as works of art worthy of a modicum of respect. While they remain literary works which retain the necessary minimum to be called books (letters, words, paper pages, binding), they nevertheless appear unsubstantial to the average understanding. Even for the more sophisticated observer, they overturn expectations in several important respects. One presupposes that something produced as a book will use the best of modern technology to produce it, rather than the lesser means typically used for ephemeral duplication; that copies of a work with the same title will have the same contents, unless it is described as a new edition; that pages in one book will not be totally interchangeable with those in another; that one kind of paper and duplication process (typeset printing) will be used more or less throughout; that, in short, there will be more to it than there is to these works by Krucenyx.

—Gerald Janecek, "Krucenyx's Autographic Books"

The experience of comprehending words incorporated into a variety of communications media reveals how they differ as extensions of literary language:

> Individual pages, prints, and paintings have the common quality of best presenting words in two-dimensional space, where layout, letter size, and white space affect the presentation and thus the comprehension of language.
>
> Theater offers live performance and thus person-to-person communication, where time-based sound and static images can compliment language.
>
> Audiotape presents words in time, so that rhythm and silences affect the reader's experience of language.
>
> For words embedded in sculpture, shape and substance are the crucial factors in enhancing language.
>
> In holograms, words can be presented one behind the other, or parts of words can be hidden from viewers, preventing them from seeing the whole in its entirety.
>
> Videotape and film resemble each other in presenting words in automatic visual sequence (though these two media differ in

All the new media, including the press, are art forms that have the power of imposing, like poetry, their own assumptions. The new media are not ways of relating us to the old "real" world: they are the real world, and they reshape what remains of the old world at will.
—Marshall McLuhan, *Explorations in Communication* (1960)

A page is an arena on which I may place any signs I consider to communicate most nearly what I have to convey; therefore, I employ, within the pocket of my publisher and the patience of my printer, typographical techniques beyond the arbitrary and constricting limits of the conventional novel.
—B. S. Johnson, *Albert Angelo* (1964)

All media are active metaphors in their power to translate experience into new forms. The spoken word was the first technology by which man was able to let go of his environment in order to graph it in a new way. Words are a kind of information retrieval that can range over the total environment and experience at high speed. Words are complex systems of metaphors and symbols that translate experience into our uttered and outered senses. They are a technology of explicitness.
—Marshall McLuhan, *Understanding Media* (1964)

other respects, video being more intimate than film, which is, like television, about mass communcation).

A computer hypertext creates fluid textual structure and is thus appropriate for narratives with varying paths; so that an interactive reader can move the story not straight from A to Z but to many variable points among and between.

Books incorporate the human process of turning the page, which means that they deal not only with sequential continuity but with cross-referencing. In books, unlike film or videotape, the reader can, on his own initiative, quickly and conveniently refer back to any particular early moment or skip ahead to any later one, even looking at both almost at once.

The introduction of a new communications medium, like videotape or holography, can at its beginning produce an instant avant-garde, creating literature unlike anything seen before.

Genuine contemporary literacy includes the capacity to read the languages of these media, as well as the words published in them (and about them in manuals). The experience of language in other media suggests that the printed page may place as great a limitation upon "imaginative writing" as syntax.

(1) Printed words are seen and not heard.

(2) Concepts are communicated by conventional words and shaped in the letters of the alphabet.

(3) Concepts should be expressed with the greatest economy—optically not phonetically.

(4) The layout of the text on the page, governed by the laws of typographical mechanics, must reflect the rhythm of the content.

(5) Plates must be used in the organization of the page according to the new visual theory: the supernaturalistic reality of the perfected eye.

(6) The continuous sequence of pages—the cinematographic book.

(7) The new book demands new writers; inkwell and quill have become obsolete.

(8) The printed page is not conditioned by space and time. The printed page and the endless number of books must be overcome.

—El Lissitzky, "The Electrolibrary" (1923)

One promise of new media for literary creation is transcending the obstacles of middlemen (aka publishers), as most offer the possibility of direct communication.

La copa de la amargura

Dos copas de acíbar á un tiempo ha bebido,
Y á cual más amarga, la patria Oriental:
Pierde á un hijo virtuoso y querido,
Y en la guerra su lauro triunfal.
Podrá bien la infausta suerte
Cambiarse y serle más fiel,
Mas su tesoro la muerte
No le devuelve cruel.
La patria fallece
Al fiero rigor,
Y le ofrece
Su dolor,
Sí
Sí,
Dolor,
¡Ay!
¡Ay!
Pesar
Y amargura,
Y cubierta de luto y tristura,
Sólo quiere por Sierra llorar.
—Francisco Acuña de Figueroa (1791-1862)

m a r c a r e l p a s o uno dos uno dos uno dos uno
dos uno c a d a c o s a u n n ú m e r o uno dos dos
disposición a uno tres tres disposición a uno cuatro
cuatro cinco cuatro cuatro pasado de uno c a d a
n ú m e r o un l u g a r un uno en uno dos
disposiciones a uno en cuatro y siete un pasado de uno
en catorce dos dos en dos y tres dos tres en cinco y
seis cuatro cuatros en ocho nueve once y doce un
cinco en diez a b s t r a c t o paso guardias
guardias va a pasar pancartas pancartas va a pasar
policías policías echar el choche a un lado de la
carretera policías policías pasó
—José Luis Castillejo, *La Política* (Zaj, 1968)

SPATIAL FORM

The American critic Joseph Frank perceived, a half-century ago, that much innovative modernist writing is "spatial" in form, as opposed to linear. Even in traditionally narrative genres, such as fiction, the representation of time is often so fragmented and disordered that the reader has trouble "following" the plot the first time through. In Frank's analysis, advanced fiction is emulating a characteristic form of modernist poetry, which favors a "spatial interweaving of images and phrases independently of any time-sequence or narrative action." As novels structured in this way recompose the chronology of the stories they tell, they force the reader to develop perceptual processes quite different from those honed on traditional fiction. Frank advised that "By continually fitting fragments together and keeping allusions in mind by reflexive reference, [the reader] can link them to their complements."

Though some old-fashioned readers (and teachers) try, at least mentally, to reorder the parts into the semblance of linear sequence, this effort is usually futile. Not only do certain temporal relationships remain persistently ambiguous, but the effort seems false to the epistemology of the work. Precisely because such writing neglects the linear representation of time, it

Skip anything you don't understand [in my Cantos] and go on till
you pick it up again. All tosh about *foreign languages* making it
difficult. The quotes are all either explained at once by repeat
or they are definitively *of* the things indicated.
—Ezra Pound, in a letter (1934)

In the direct experience of fiction, continuity is the center of
our attention; our later memory, what I call the possession of
it, tends to become discontinuous. Our attention shifts from the
sequence of incidents to another focus: a sense of what the work
of ficton was all *about*.
—Northrop Frye, "Myth, Fiction, and Displacement" (1961)

A story is no longer a story when words are reduced to bare
necessities. Time is cancelled out in the process of exploring it,
when the quest for a perfect recurrence, a coming and going in
time, is achieved by means of pure prose, of writing reduced to
its essence.
—Henri Lefebvre, *Everyday Life in the Modern World* (1968)

In any age how to read and how to write are complementary
terms, and the reading of the Pound Era, like the writing,
discerns patterns of fiction and gathers meaning from
nonconsecutive arrays. We can tell one page of *Ulysses* from
another at a glance; to our grandfathers they would have seemed
as featureless as pages from a telephone directory.
—Hugh Kenner, *The Pound Era* (1971)

The tendency of literature has been to escape itself, to subvert
or transcend its form, to re-imagine imagination, and, as it
were, to create a state of unmediated literary awareness.
—Ihab Hassan, *Paracriticisms* (1975)

tends to portray life in process, without specific beginnings or ends; in this respect, it is truly utopian.

Since "what happens next" is not a consequential matter, it would instead be wiser for the reader to disregard chronological concerns—to take the story as it is, letting it engage him or her directly, and even reading serendipitously around a book, rather than directly through it—just as a viewer no longer needs to reconstruct a detailed representation of space to understand a cubist painting. Major works of contemporary literature create an impression, an aura, an "afterimage," apart from the details of plot and subject; and it is these encompassing qualities that the reader absorbs and especially remembers.

A painting need not be read from "beginning to end." Nor need most modern-music compositions. Nor need the pages of *Finnegans Wake*, typically, be read in numerical sequence. Whether the reader has examined every page is no longer a measure of whether he has "finished" the book. A work of literature is not necessarily a channel that progresses in a single direction. It can be understood as a field that is read from several angles.

This essay of mine (that you are now reading) need not be read sequentially, although certain advantages are perhaps gained by doing so.

When a critic deals with a work of literature, the most natural thing for him to do is to freeze it, to ignore its movement in time and look at it as a completed pattern of words, with all its parts existing simultaneously.
—Northrop Frye, "Myth, Fiction, and Displacement" (1961)

The musical conception of form, that is to say the understanding that you can use form as a musician uses sound, that you can select motives of form from the forms before you, that you can recombine and recolour them and "organise" them into a new form—that conception, this state of mental activity, brings with it a great joy and refreshment. I do not wish to convert anyone. I simply say that a certain sort of pleasure is available to anyone who wants it.
—Ezra Pound, "Vorticism" (1915)

I begin, then, with the assumption that Ives wrote pictorial music—music based largely on relationships that are simultaneous, reciprocal, and reflective in nature rather than successive, sequential, and unidirectional. It is in this sense that I say that there relationships are primarily spatial in nature rather than temporal. If this music is approached in these terms, I think that much that may otherwise seem puzzling in it becomes more readily comprehensible.
—Robert P. Morgan, in *An Ives Celebration* (1977)

You might if you chose develop any part of the picture, for the idea of sequence does not really exist as far as the author is concerned. Sequence arises only because words have to be written one after the other on consecutive pages, just as the reader's mind must have time to go through the book, at least the first time he reads it. Time and sequence cannot exist in the author's mind because no time element and no space element had ruled the initial vision. If the mind were constructed on optional

Here and elsewhere, modernist fiction prepares its readers to make those perceptual readjustments necessary to comprehend subsequent new fiction. In reading such works (unlike detective stories), what is principally remembered is not narrative sequence but a sense, first, of thematic interests and, then, images of both characters and the atmosphere in which they move, in addition to prose style and overall structures—qualities that the attentive reader comprehends bit by bit. It is those qualities, rather than anything dependent upon sequential narrative, that the modernist novel tries especially to communicate; so that "spatial form" becomes a means entwined in an epistemological end.

It was Guy Davenport, a very literate writer, who observed of Stan Brakhage, a very literary filmmaker, that the latter's *Anticipation of the Night* (1958) contains "a succession of images that do not tell a story but define a state of mind."

The publishers of Erich Auerbach's classic book on changing literary representation, *Mimesis* (1946), should invite avant-garde critics to write a successor to Auerbach's concluding chapter on Virginia Woolf's *To the Lighthouse* (1927). (My choice would be stories in Gertrude Stein's *Geography and Plays*, which was incidentally published five years before Woolf's book, just as Stein was born eight years before Woolf.)

lines and if a book could be read in the same way as a painting is taken in by the eye, that is without the bother of working form left to right and without the absurdity of beginnings and ends—this would be the ideal way of appreciating a novel, for thus the author saw it at the moment of its conception.
—Vladimir Nabokov, "The Art of Literature and Commonsense," *Lectures on Literature* (1980).

By reducing the text to a minimum (syllables, letters, line), Kruchonykh indeed achieved one goal, that of simultaneity. Such a page of "text" need not be read sequentially in linear time, but can be taken in at a glance and absorbed by the same process of free visual exploration used in studying a painting.
—Gerald Janecek, *The Look of Russian Literature* (1984)

"POST-MODERN"

It has been fashionable to speak of current art as "post-modern," which implies that we are now into a period that should be understood as coming *after* "modernism." However, this new term is scarcely appropriate, because a genuine post-modernism would represent either a departure from modernism or a repudiation of it. Harold Rosenberg defined the latter possibility as "a relaxation, a stopping short, or even a return to a state preceding modernist excitement." He could not discern this happening now. Nor can I.

"Modernism," remember, is a term for art and thought that decidedly depart from nineteenth century practice. In most arts, modernism began after World War I with the conscious perception, within the community of thoughtful people, of activities drastically different from their immediate precursors. "Modernism" became synonymous with "the tradition of the new"—with the history of avant-garde art.

In fuller retrospect, we can identify earlier works that realize equally radical departures, such as the compositions of Charles Ives, the plays and fictions of Alfred Jarry, the prophetic books of William Blake, and the poetry of Walt Whitman. Nonetheless, "modernism," as we commonly understand it, began in the nineteenth century, with certain perceptible changes in art.

Modernism includes more than just art and literature. By now it includes almost the whole of what is truly alive in our culture.
—Clement Greenberg, "Modernist Painting" (1965)

During the period there was a deepening cultural crisis, and a deepening literary response, going from an advance-guard of subject matter to an advance-guard of form to an advance-guard of questioning the worth of the art itself and its relation to the audience.
—Paul Goodman, "Advance-Guard Writing in America: 1900-50" (1951)

Whether because the contemporary situation is no longer thought to be manageable by ideas (as the vanguardists assumed it was) or because society has become too disillusioned, or too level-headed, to be taken in by utopian fantasies, post-modernism has no use for vanguards. In fact, the essential condition of "post-modern" may be a "period without vanguards."
—Harold Rosenberg, "Inquest into Modernism" (1978)

Especially in certain literary tendencies, Anglo-American extremism is among the most typical and significant expressions of the contemporary avant-garde spirit. But Anglo-American avant-gardism compensates for this by being less theoretical and self-conscious, more instinctive and empirical.
—Renato Poggioli, *The Theory of the Avant-Garde* (1963)

Late-Modernism in architecture. . . is pragmatic and technocratic in its social ideology and from about 1960 takes many of the stylistic ideas and values of Modernism to an extreme in order to resuscitate a dull (or clichéd) language.
—Charles Jencks, *What Is Post-Modernism?* (1986)

The best works of modernism rank among the great human achievements of mankind.

Theoretically, this so-called "post-modernism" should be a development so clear-cut that historians of art and literature could draw a line between the two periods—a line at least as definite as that separating "modernism" from pre-modernism. However, this dividing line is not drawn and, in my judgment, cannot be.

Besides, "post" is a petty prefix, both today and historically, for major movements are defined in their own terms, rather than by their relation to something else. The only *post* in my dictionary of art history is "Post-Impressionism," which the editors, Peter and Linda Murray, characterize as "a vague term" to define "either a return to a more formal conception of art or a new stress on the importance of the subject." My music dictionary has "post-romanticism" to define patently decadent, post-Wagnerian developments (e.g., Mahler). No genuine avant-garde artist would want to be "post" anything.

"Post-impressionism" has a certain validity as a characterization of what came after a certain painterly style; but since the epithet "modern" is more general than particular, "post-modern" is yet more vague. "Post-industrialism" has some usefulness as a definition of a culture that is heavily, if not predominantly, electronic, because it defines a discernible transition from

A decade ago, we began to hear the prefix "post" applied to everything in art that had managed to sustain itself on the market for longer than two years. It is worth recalling that this well-worn prefix was once applied to the term "impressionism" by Roger Fry in order to categorize what itinerant painters like Van Gogh and Gauguin were trying to do. In recent years, the more prevalent nomenclature is that of 'postmodernism' (just one step ahead of 'post-painterly-abstraction')—a term which has created a good deal of ambiguity among critics. One source for the term "post-modernism" finds its etiology in a style of architecture that was conceived either as a reaction to Mies or as some fanciful variation upon the look of austerity in recent buildings. Soon, however, the term slid into the vocabularly of arts critics, particularly journalists who tired of seeing everything as "pluralism." Its lack of generic connotation became too vague and too generalized to be of much benefit or consolation.
—Robert C. Morgan, "The Delta of Modernism" (1981)

Early modernism tended toward fascism, later modernism toward anarchism.
—Frank Kermode, "Modernisms" (1966)

Theory *on its own terms* must grasp modernism before it can deal with subsequent developments, whether these be formulations of historical periodization, literary movements, or trans-genre aesthetic categories. Thus for modernism to be rationalized *its most extreme manifestations* must be theorizable. In order for contemporary theory to proceed with business, in other words, it must first kill off the avant-garde.
—Harry Polkinhorn, "The Death and Resurrection of the Avant-Garde: Subjectivity and Photographic Imagery" (1989)

the mechanical age to something else; but why not call a spade "a spade" and use *electronic*, rather than "post-shovel"?

It is more apt to regard advanced art and writing today as extensions of earlier modernist developments. Even if new literature echoes Gertrude Stein, say, more than Thomas Mann, it still echoes modernism—the more radical fringes of modernism, to be sure, but modernism nonetheless. In addition to drawing upon earlier innovation, even today's most extreme art also honors the modernist values of experiment, mediumistic integrity, complexity, subtlety, difficulty. Artworks that are currently considered "innovative" neither close modernism nor transcend it.

Some "post-modern" art implicitly repudiates modernism, but it is customarily classed as *retrograde*. None of it is consequential enough to earn a place in the pantheon of art history. It is not "post-modern" but *post-mortem*.

YE CARPETTE KNYGHTE

I have a horse—a ryghte good horse—
Ne doe I envie those
Who scoure ye plaine in headie course,
Tyll soddaine on theyre nose
They lyghte wyth unexpected force—
It ys—a horse of clothes.

I have a saddel—"Say'st thou soe?
With styrruppes, Knyghte, to boote?"
I sayde not that—I answere "Noe"—
Yt lacketh such, I woot—
It ys a mutton-saddel, loe!
Parte of ye fleecie brute.

I have a bytte—ayghte good bytte—
As schall bee seene in tyme.
Ye jawe of horse yt wyll not fytte—
Yts use ys more sublyme.
Fayre Syr, how deemest though of yt?
Yt ys—thys bytte of rhyme.

—Lewis Carroll

EDUCATION

Literature is a "teaching machine" that particularly prepares its students to read more literature. (A machine, we remember, is "a structure consisting of a framework and various fixed and moving parts for doing some kind of work.") Literature depends for its pedagogic success upon the fact that running words before one's eyes is, for many people, first of all a pleasure.

Since literary innovation completely revamps our tastes in previous literature, one byproduct of experimental writing is a reinterpretation of the literary past, inevitably to emphasize certain previously neglected precursors. New works shine different lights on past writers. After one has appreciated *Finnegans Wake*, for instance, Lewis Carroll seems the most interesting Victorian writer, and Lawrence Sterne and William Blake the masters of the eighteenth century. After a reader has submerged himself or herself deeply in contemporary avant-garde writing, the Russian futurists seem more interesting than the English Romantics, art criticism more fertile than literary criticism, Moholy-Nagy and Kurt Schwitters more suggestive than artists who specialized in only one medium, and the essays of both Ezra Pound and T. S. Eliot more pertinent than their poetry. One also prefers Gertrude Stein to William Faulkner, E. E. Cummings

The eye *likes* certain plainnesses, certain complexities, certain arrangements, certain varieties, certain incitements, certain reliefs and suspensions.

It likes these things irrespective of whether or not they form a replica of known objects.
—Ezra Pound, "The Vortographs" (1917)

Art is a series of creations couched in a language peculiar to itself.
—André Malraux, *The Imaginary Museum* (1953)

History has imposed upon the avant-garde the duty not only of disinterestedly cultivating art and ideas but of educating and leading an aimless body of Philistine taste and opinion.
—Richard Chase, "The Fate of the Avant-Garde" (1957)

The technique of art is to make objects 'unfamiliar,' to make forms difficult, to increase the difficulty and length of perception because the process of perception is an aesthetic end in itself and must be prolonged. Art is a way of experiencing the artfulness of an object: the object is not important.
—Victor Shklovsky, "Art as Technique" (1917)

All original composition—classical, standard, or advance-guard—occurs at the limits of the artist's knowledge, feeling and technique. Being a spontaneous art, it risks, supported by what one has already grown up to, something unknown.
—Paul Goodman, "Advance-Guard Writing in America: 1900-50" (1951)

to Robert Frost, Wyndham Lewis to D.H. Lawrence, and Dada to Surrealism. *Alice in Wonderland* is still literature, while *Middlemarch* is by now sociology, history, or a public-television serial.

We go to school to learn to read writing we cannot read by ourselves, whether that writing be literature or scientific exposition. Education gives readers a taste for books previously unavailable to them, as well as a quick and sure distaste for books that need not be read.

Literature teaches us not only how to read but how to reread.

Art offers more than pleasure or distraction; it offers perceptual education, increasing our capacities for esthetic attention.

Useful literature becomes a machine teaching us how to perceive words in ways we have not done before. Perceptual enhancement is one fundamental human value of art.

The quality of a man's life nowadays depends largely on the quality of what he reads. . . . So a diet of the second-rate blunts one's capacity for genuine feeling and disables the mind for digesting new and invigorating ideas.
—Denys Thompson, *Reading and Discrimination* (1934)

KNOWLEDGE

Knowledge of past art is the most essential preparation for perceiving originality in the present. Only by knowing thoroughly "what has already been done" can one acknowledge what is genuinely new. Especially after reading a carload of conventional novels and realizing their limitations, one becomes ready, if not eager, to appreciate true innovation.

The use of language presupposes an audience that knows what words mean. The creation of literature depends upon the existence of an audience familiar with literary discourses. The creation of experimental writing presupposes a yet smaller audience sufficiently literate to appreciate innovative differences, as well as understanding the relation of innovative work to its tradition.

Similarly, the experimental writer differs from the conventional one in the former's familiarity with the ways in which imaginative literature no longer need be written. Anyone who nowadays writes sentimental fiction, say, by that fact reveals either cynicism or limited literacy. The adventurous reader similarly differs from the conventional one.

From past literature, the derivative poet learns what to write; the inventive poet, what not to write.

Newness is a constant conception. It exists only in the difference between things, and it is not visible in consciousness if, as directed by traditional esthetics, a work is seen 'for itself alone.'
—Michael Kirby, "The Aesthetics of the Avant-Garde" (1969)

Actually the composer has come to distrust his inspiration because it is not really as innocent as it was supposed to be, but rather conditioned by a tremendous body of recollection, tradition, training, and experience.
—Ernst Krenek, "Extents and Limits of Serial Techniques," *The Musical Quarterly* (1960)

Conversely, a general understanding of the varieties of form in art, derived from observation and reasoning, will aid in further observation. The fact of having encountered similar kinds of art or qualities in art before, of having singled them out for attention and given them a name and a place in the scheme of things, makes it easier to deal with them in a later situation. One is less bewildered, quicker to see how the present work of art resembles and differs from previous ones. One has become a skilled, powerful observer, like a man at a football game who understands the game and its finer points, in contrast to a foreigner who sees only meaningless running and gesturing.
—Thomas Munro, "The Morphology of Art as a Branch of Aesthetics" (1954)

In order to experience and participate actively in all the aspects of contemporary literature the student must be acquainted through records and concerts with
(1) the tendencies of contemporary composers such as Stravinsky, Bartok, Schoenberg, Hindemith, Krenek, Milhaud, Copland, Varèse and others. Their works offer an enlightening analogy to modern literature as well as to contemporary paint-

The contemporary visual artist Robert Motherwell once remarked that the contemporary artist carries the history of modern art around in his head, and the possession of such mental baggage is essential not only for the avoidance of plagiarism but also for the development of discriminating avant-garde perception. To both artist and audience, knowlege of precursors is a prerequiste for the experience of historically authentic surprise. An illiterate, by contrast, is likely either to miss significant innovation or to be fooled by false advertising (which opportunistically exploits ignorance).

Apollinaire: "It is by the element of surprise, by the important place it assigns to surprise, that the new spirit is distinguished from all earlier artistic and literary movements." The spectator's pleasure in the experience of surprise is quite different from the satisfaction to be derived from observing the fulfillment of a literary convention.

The difference between the artist's filling forms and inventing them is comparable to the divergence between the spectator's appreciating a conventional realization and his experience of surprise.

Knowledge provides context that informs current experience. Without a familiarity with past works of art, it would be impossible to comprehend, say, the significance of inferential

ing. Like cubism and constructivism, the modern polyphonic music, with its interwoven, intricate traits, the experiments of the brutists ("noise-ists" pioneered by the futurist Luigi Russolo, 1913), will lead to an analysis of literary equivalents; to the

(2) simultaneists, futurists, as they appear in the work of Guillaume Apollinaire, F. T. Marinetti, Vladimir Mayakovski and from there to the

(3) expressionists and proto-surrealists: August Stramm, Lajos Kassak, Franz Kafka, Yvan Goll, Ezra Pound, Gertrude Stein, Jean Cocteau, Blaise Cendrars, Bert Brecht, etc., to the

(4) dadaists: Tristan Tzara, Jean Arp, Hugo Ball, Richard Hulsenbeck, Kurt Schwitters, Ribemont-Dessaignes, etc., to the

(5) surrealists and

(6) James Joyce.

—L. Moholy-Nagy, *Vision in Motion* (1947)

What makes the artist is that in his youth he was more deeply moved by his visual experiences of works of art than by that of the things they represent—and perhaps of nature as a whole.

—André Malraux, *The Imaginary Museum* (1953)

(aka conceptual) art, such as John Cage's 4'33"
which is superficially a presentation of no-sound
(or, more profoundly, incidental noise) in a context where music is expected, or, for another
example, Marcel Duchamp's history of meaning-
ful inactions.

Especially to understand innovative writing, readers should know other arts as well. One
reason is that experimental writers like to discover whether an idea developed in another art
can be applied to their own; indeed, that procedure exemplifies creative processes that are, at
base, truly experimental. Unless one is familiar
with minimalism, say, in painting, he is liable to
miss its possible uses and effects in writing.

Conversely, a knowledge of modernist writing helps one's appreciation of the other arts.
Finnegans Wake is probably the most appropriate
precursor, as well as the most effective sensi-
tizer, to multiple serialization in contemporary
music.

L'Inquiétude

```
1 " 23456789  10 11 12 :  :  :  :  :  : -TTTTTTT—Qh
                Dragnnnnnnnnnnnnnnnnnnnnnnnnn
                !
(Petite)        $ !Droooooooooooooooooooooo.
                !
                !
                PI!TY
```

I'll see you again soon, yes, sooon.
Thought : (sooner than you think) soune or suun !

Collender 1920

Wetch by time

```
 .  .  .  .  .  .  .  .  .  .   .  .  .  .  .  .
 1  2  3  4  5  6  7  8  9  10  S  M  T  W  T  F  S
```

—Man Ray (1890-1976)

TECHNIQUES

In art, as in sex, much depends upon techniques that are acquired through experience. For the practice of writing, the most useful acquisition initially involves a mastering of basic procedures—how to write sentences, construct paragraphs, observe forms, organize perceptions, etc. This can be done in an academic setting, or in a situation of apprenticeship, or by concentrated personal study "on the streets," so to speak. The operational assumpton is that these techniques enable an aspiring artist to impose the intelligence of effective forms upon "talent" and "invention."

At mimimum, techniques comprise an arsenal of options for lessening the inevitable resistances between an artist's imagination and his or her chosen medium—between the mental desire and its material realization. An idiot can be a good athlete, even in sports requiring intelligence (e.g., American football), if he assimilates those techniques that will, with a maximum of physical effort and psychological concentration, enable him to perform intelligently. Mastery of superior technique can also enable inferior minds to produce intelligent writing, precisely because effective form marshals their mental material.

Diction refers to the selection of words, the "vocabulary" used in a work of literature. The arrangement of these words into sentences and larger units constitutes a *style,* which is a characteristic manner of expression in prose or verse—it is *how* a speaker or writer says whatever he says.
—M. H. Abrams, *A Glossary of Literary Terms* (1957)

Merely to convey thought is not an art, but a craft, if not a trade. Over and above the desire to communicate thought, there is for the artist as writer the desire to make it prevail in the minds of others; in short, art is a means of power. To express himself is not enough; he wishes to impress himself. Style is only the device adopted by great writers to make their powers more attractive than repulsive. Style is power made gracious.
—A. R. Orage, quoted by Margaret Anderson, "The Art of Prose," *Prose* (Fall, 1970)

I began to publish enough, and not too slowly, to justify my hopes for success, and as I continued, I made a most perplexing discovery—namely, that for all his conscious concern with technique, a writer did not so much create the novel as he was created by the novel. That is, one did not make an arbitrary gesture when one sought to write. And when I say that the novelist is created by the novel, I mean to remind you that fictional techniques are not a mere set of objective tools, but something much more intimate: a way of feeling, of seeing, and of expressing one's sense of life. And the process of acquiring technique is a process of modifying one's responses, of learning to see and feel, to hear and observe, to evoke and evaluate the images of memory and of summoning up and directing the imagination; of learning to conceive of human values in ways which have been established by the great writers who have developed and extended the art. And perhaps the writer's greatest freedom, as an artist, lies precisely in his possession

An aspiring poet is someone who is assimilating the traditions and techniques of poetry. Artistic growth is measured initially by an increasing mastery of extant forms, and then by an ability to generate artwork with personal signature.

As different sports emphasize different techniques, so do different literary genres; and even within the techniques indigenous to a certain genre, different styles or "positions" emphasize particular techniques. Whereas one kind of fiction depends upon characterization, another emphasizes heightened prose, a third formal invention. "Technique," according to Gertrude Stein, "is not so much a thing of form and style as the way that form and style came and how it can come again." (Technique is thus a true mechanism—a generative system that exploits human talent to produce certain ends.)

Without a mastery of those fundamental techniques, the aspiring artist, like the aspiring athlete, can hardly begin to play the game successfully. Lacking technique, both artist and athlete will otherwise feel oppressed by desires that cannot find expression—at least not in forms they find satisfactory.

As one learns to write initially by reading, so it is by rereading that one learns to rewrite, as well as how not to rewrite, and by rewriting that one learns for oneself the development of

of technique; for it is through technique that he comes to possess and express the meaning of his life.
—Ralph Ellison, *Shadow and Act* (1964)

Art has its impotents and its imposters—if fewer than in the field of love. As in the case of love its nature is often confused with the pleasure it may give; but, like love, it is not itself a pleasure but a passion, and involves a break/away from the world's values in favor of a value of its own, obsessive and all-powerful. The artist has need of others who share his passion and he can live fully only in their company.
—André Malraux, *The Voices of Silence* (1953).

linguistic signature. What happens after mastering the basic technique is the true measure of inspired artistry.

THICK FOLIAGE

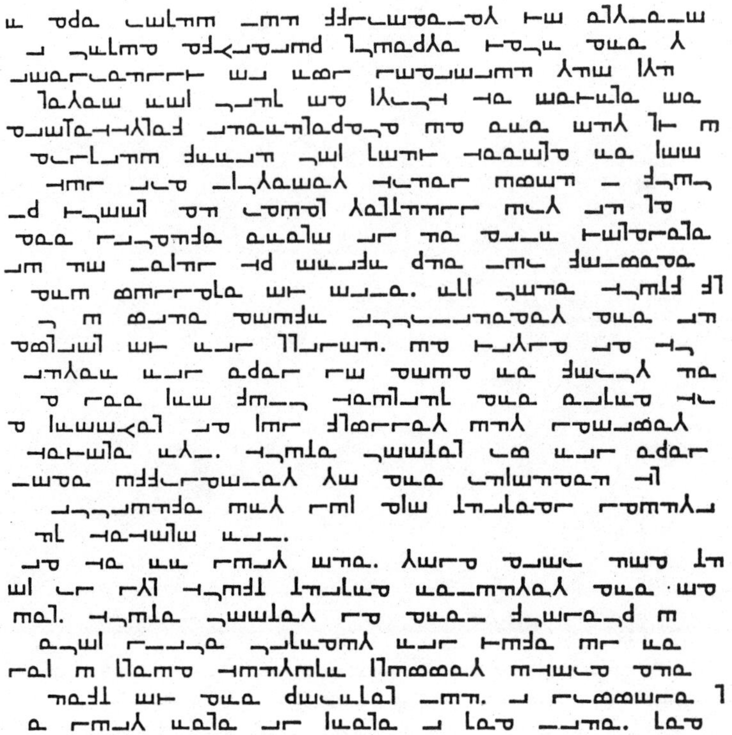

It's no use! No use! No use! Mrs Newton said to herself. How-

—Guy de Cointet (1976)

PHILISTINISM

In protesting resistances to the dissemination of their work, experimental writers are advised to blame the amorphous public; but it is really more appropriate to excoriate the middlemen—publishers, reviewers, and booksellers—who stand between new art and its likely public.

Decidedly innovative writers inevitably fall into a quarrel with other writers. In a remarkably percipient reformulation of the identity of philistinism, the art critic Leo Steinberg noted that, "Whenever there appears an art that is truly new and original, the men who denounce it first and loudest are artists. Obviously, because they are the most engaged. No critic, no outraged bourgeois, can match an artist's passion in repudiation. . . . Therefore, instead of repeating the charge that only academic painters spurn the new, why not reverse the charge? Any man becomes academic by virtue of, or with respect to, what he rejects?"

If "critics" dislike a new artist's work, it may not be particularly good; but if artists dislike him or her as well and, surer yet, if they publicly denounce his or her work and, surer yet, try to exclude it from professional spoils, then it is probably exceptionally original. Nothing measures the power of a new style more surely than

The writer who defines his audience by its limitations is
indulging in the unforgivable arrogance.
—Lionel Trilling, "The Function of the Little Magazine"(1946)

But so far every attack on the "formalist" aspect of modernist
painting and sculpture has worked out as an attack at the same
time on superior artistic standards.
—Clement Greenberg, "Necessity of 'Formalism'" (1971)

It is very difficult to make people understand the *impersonal*
indignation that a decay of writing can cause men who understand what it implies, and the end whereto it leads. It is almost
impossible to express any degree of such indignation without
being called 'embittered,' or something of that sort.
—Ezra Pound, *ABC of Reading* (1934)

A work of art lives on its form, not on its material; the essential
grace it emanates springs from its structure, from its organ-
ism. The structure forms the properly artistic part of the
work, and on it aesthetic and literary criticism should concentrate. If too much stress is laid on the subject of a painting or
a poem, sensitive nerves smell the Philistine.
—José Ortega y Gasset, "Notes on the Novel" (1925)

The negative critic, when not simply outraged, usually proceeds by identifying the absence of some single feature of the
new work that he or she regards as an indispensable attribute
of all genre members or, alternatively, the presence of a
feature that is antithetical to such an attribute. In fact this
indispensable attribute is almost inevitably merely a marked
feature of all members of some favored subgenre. So for Robert
Frost or Allen Tate "formal versification" was the indispensable attribute of poetry, for Stanley Cavell pervasive "compo-

the extent to which self-conscious establishments dismiss and exclude it.

In my observation, it is not professional editors but other poets who *resist* (rather than just neglect) the publication of experimental literature; it is not one's superiors but one's peers who envy experimental work (and by their envy define themselves as competitors, rather than superiors). That explains why contributors to the current avant-gardes in poetry and fiction are completely excluded from all the periodicals and anthologies edited by practicing poets and novelists, not to mention grants and awards. (And such exclusion becomes, of course, a measure of the possible cultural threat of such work.)

The commissars of cultural commerce, who control the populous channels of communication, subscribe to the principle of precedent, whose fundamental rule is that nothing succeeds more surely than semblances of past success. While aspiring writers desirous of immediate prosperity are encouraged to imitate the currently fashionable formulas, there is nothing, absolutely nothing, that the scrupulous avant-gardist wants to resemble least.

One crucial reason why innovative literature encounters more obstacles than, say, advanced visual art in overcoming marketplace resistance is that book publishing is a wholesale business while art-dealing is primarily retail—

sitional choice" the indispensable attribute of music, while for Michael Fried the "literalness" of Minimal Art was antithetical to art, or at least to "modernist" "painting."
—David Antin, "The Stranger at the Door" (1986)

Paris Dada . . . was based on a contempt for bourgeois taste but not on any real opposition to bourgeois society.
—John Willett, *Art & Politics in the Weimar Period* (1972)

the book publisher necessarily thinks in terms of
selling an important new work to at least several
thousand customers while dealers in new paintings and sculptures think in terms of only one
likely collector.

x k k x k x k x k x x k x k x k x k x x k x k x k x
k x k x k x k x k x k x k x k x k x k x k x k x k x
k x k x k x k x k x k x k k x k x k x k k x k x k x
k x k x k x k x x k x x k x k x k x x k x k x k x k
x k x k x k x k x k x k x k k x k x k x k k x k x k
x x k x k x k x k x x k x x k x k x x k x k x k x k
x k x k x k x k x x k x k x k x k x k x k x k x k x
k x k x k x k x k x k x x k x k x k x k x k x k k x
k x k x k x k x k x x k x k x k x k x k x k x k k x
k x k x k x k x k x x k x k x k x k x k x k x k k x
k x k x k x k x k x x k x k x k x k x k x k x k k x
k x k x k x k x k x x k x k x k x k x k x k x k k x
k x k x k x k x k x x k x k x k x k x k x k x k k x
k x k x k x k x k x x k x k x k x k x k x k x k k x
k x k x k x x k x k x k x k k x k x x k x k x k k x

—José Luis Castillejo, *El Libro de las Dieciocho Letras* (1972)

REPUTATION

An artist initiates his or her "reputation" by showing new work to friends; and if one of them likes the new work and in turn tells his friends about the work he likes, that person becomes the initial engine in a burgeoning process. Should this admirer be influential, because his spoken opinions are persuasive, say, or because he has access to publicizing media (or he has students), then other people will reiterate this initial praise, which will in turn be communicated to expanding circles of possible admirers. A growing reputation proceeds from inner circles to outer circles.

At this point the reputation will probably have its detractors, especially if the new work is perceived to be "different" or "threatening." Though these disparaging critics may make considerable noise, their negative opinion does not really hamper the development of a reputation. Nothing in art is "hated" unless it is loved by someone else. (The worst fate is being ignored.) Indeed, vociferous hate inadvertently gives a new art publicity, which induces people to pay attention to what they would otherwise neglect.

By this point the further growth of an artist's eminence depends less upon who deprecates his work than upon those who like it, and then upon whether the latter can communicate their enthusiasm to yet larger circles of possible admirers. The measure of a reputation's decline

So much literary criticism and theory and so much of the best
has been written by the men of letters. Often, whether consciously or not, they have written their general theories as a
comment on their own best performances in poetry, and on the
kinds of poetry which were most dear to them.
—W. K. Wimsatt, Jr., and Cleanth Brooks, *Literary Criticism: A
Short History* (1957)

If total strangers write to you and say that they got something
out of this, then the money thing is secondary. I think anybody,
anybody, if given the choice, would always take the privilege of
having his work wanted by other people, rather than the
privilege of having more money than anybody.
—*Conversations with Nelson Algren* (1964)

Serious art is unpopular at its birth. But it ultimately forms
the mass culture.
—Ezra Pound, *Impact* (1960)

There are two kinds of elitism: the one is a belief that there is
an elite or natural aristocracy of some kind who comprise the
few who are truly capable of appreciating a serious cultural
communication. This is not, of course, a democratic attitude and
those who believe in a democracy are properly uncomfortable
with such an attitude, which is usually described as "snob-
bish." The other is the elitism which comes from the idea that
this is an imperfect world, that our education and experience
are wanting, and that in such a world it is simply not realistic
to expect everybody to be able to discern, equally well, the more
arcane points of cultural experience.

There is a fortunate elite, a person feels, who can do so,
an elite which normally does not coincide with the worlds of
privilege, social, fashionable, moneyed or even educational
(since education is assumed to be flawed), and this elite has the

is not the existence of detractors but the absence of advocates. As long as someone is telling someone else about an artist's work, his or her reputation will survive.

Most serious readers trust friends of similar taste before they listen to anyone else. Most of all, they trust themselves. Nothing should persuade you to read more of an author's books than your liking one of them.

Ideally, a reputation is passed from peers to professional observers, such as serious critics and art historians, and then to publicists who in turn introduce it to a larger audience. Artists who are picked up by publicists before they win the admiration of their peers are rarely accepted by critics and historians, and the fact that this *serious* recognition is forbidden them often makes them publicly bitter and splenetic about "the critics."

The commercial publisher believes that literary success can be bought. He pays not only for advertisements but for publicists who solicit the attention of book reviewers and media executives. Nonetheless, for all the machinery of literary power that the publicists appear to have at their command, they nearly always fail. For every promotional success—for every John Updike or Susan Sontag, say—there are scores of losers (and a legion of commercially published writers who once believed that, if their work were suf-

moral obligation to share its findings and experience, to share and to test them, as it were, on the world outside itself and see if they can make their way into ever-larger numbers of people, or, if they cannot, to look for something else which can. This is the natural world of the trend-setters, of those who perform, not by fashion but by consistently sharing their findings, the "research and development" function in cultural experience. The concept of an avant-garde is inherent in such a model.
—Dick Higgins, "Five Myths of Postmodernism" (1989)

Just as the Abstract Expressionists explored the medium for its own sake, the avant-garde of the Seventies explored communication and the exchange of esthetic information, for its own sake. They focused their attention upon the distribution and distortion of the artist. This distortion is entropy.
—John Held, Jr., in *A Critical Assembling* (1980)

There is a dilemma in *any* high standard of living in a profit economy. I am referring to the embarrassing truth that the best things in life are free—things like friendly competitive sports, friendly gambling, love-making and sex, solitary study and reading, contemplation of nature and cosmos, art-working, music, religion. . . .
—Paul Goodman, "Leisure and Work" (1959)

I think often of my earlier work and what it has cost me not to have been clear. I acknowledge I have moved chaotically about refusing and rejecting most things, seldom accepting values and acknowledging anything because I early recognized the futility of acquisitive understanding and at the same time rejected religious dogmatism. My whole life has been spent (so far) in seeking to place a value upon experience and the objects of experience that would satisfy my sense of inclusiveness with-

ficiently publicized, they too could become as famous as Saul Bellow or, maybe, Jay McInerny).

Every art world has a graveyard filled with "fly-by-nights"—bright yesterday, dim today, gone tomorrow. If an artist wants a personal achievement, it would be wise for him to avoid familiar ground; if he wants commercial success, he should rub his head (and heart and soul) in it.

Avant-garde writing usually wins the loyal enthusiasm not of the powers-that-be but the powers-to-be, which is to say succeeding generations.

What is envied most in the community of art is not money, which everyone knows is a false measure, but reputation, which is the true coin of the professional realm. Whereas money can be earned, reputation ultimately cannot be bought with anything except work that an increasingly larger sophisticated public perceives as indisputably first class. Commercial publishers may marshall their employees to create the illusion of literary importance in something that they are currently trying to sell; but unless that praise is echoed in literary criticism or art history, it is mere exaggeration that will disappear when the advertising/promotion budget runs dry.

Writers who owe their eminence to the promotions of noisy publishers often envy those who have earned their eminence without adver-

out redundancy—completeness, lack of frustration with the liberty of choice.
—William Carlos Williams, *Spring and All* (1923)

I want to defend literature. It's a poor man's art. You can think, even when you can't feel comfortable among the cigarred princes and the knockkneed venerables in miniskirts who run our visual arts scene. You can write when you can't afford the fancy poncy materials to make art-canvas, silkscreens and the right kind of paint. You reach people who can't afford to hang de Koonings, Oldenburgs or Sol LeWitts.
—Dick Higgins, "Seen, Heard, and Understood" (1972)

tising; for the former fears that once his publisher loses interest (or his books are no longer profitable, or the reins of executive power change hands), they will disappear from public view. For similar reasons, those writers whose eminence is based upon the position they hold (e. g., editing a literary journal or regular appearance in a prominent magazine) have visible trouble acknowledging eminence earned without position. They feel, as they sometimes say, "threatened" not just by such eminence *per se* but by the possibility that it can be earned without "playing the game."

Literature is perhaps the last unregulated free-market in the western world. Although governments may bestow beneficence upon a select few, such spoils are nearly always viewed skeptically within the community of discriminating readers. Just as governments do not "make" literary reputations in the Western world, so they scarcely influence the reading habits of literate people. Commercial publishers are even less successful, as only a small percentage of their beneficiaries survive the machinery of rapid remaindering and classifying as "out of print."

Many artists become temporarily famous for the wrong reason—spokesmanship for a perceptible fad, the promotions of their sponsors, personal connections; but the truth is that in-

DUET

art of my dart
arrow of my marrow
butter of my abutter
bode of my abode
cope of my scope
curry of my scurry
den of my eden
do of my ado
ember of my member
eel of my feel
fort of my effort
flexibility of my inflexibility
go of my ego
gain of my again
hence of my whence
him of my whim
inky of my dinky
inter of my hinter
jog of my ajog
johnny o of my o johnny o
kipper of my skipper
kin of my skin
licker of my flicker
lapstick of my slapstick
mission of my emission
motion of my emotion
nip of my snip
now of my enow
oiler of my toiler
orpheus of my morpheus

trinsic in any community of discriminating people, whether sports fans or literate readers, is a collective critical machine that insures that *eventually* the cream rises to the top.

port of my sport

patter of my spatter

quash of my squash

quiescence of my acquiscence

raving of my craving

ream of my cream

scent of my ascent

swan of my aswan

tiff of my stiff

top motion of my stop motion

unction of my function

urging of my purging

vent of my event

vocative of my evocative

well of my swell

wallow-tail of my swallow-tail

x-factor of my ex-factor

x of my ax

ye of my aye

y of my my

zip zap zoff of my o zip o zap o zoff

zim zam zoom of my o zim o zam o zoom

—Emmett Williams (b.1925)

SELECTIVITY

The cruelest process in art is the selectivity that informs its communication. Out of the many who practice, only a few are awarded the opportunity to be acclaimed.

Publishers select from the manuscripts available to them; book reviewers select from the publications that are sent to them.

Bookstore managers, even in more sophisticated shops, select from the titles offered them, and customers select from the merchandize available in the stores they choose to visit.

Readers select when they read or reread one book of the many on their shelves and select again when they recommend a book to other readers, who in turn discriminate among recommendations.

Historians of art and literature memorialize reputations by selecting from the hundreds that have some critical currency, and both readers and teachers exercise preferences in historians.

Though thousands of artists are working at any particular time, the annals of Art History contain remarkably few names; and not only is membership in this top echelon continually changing, but the honor rolls get shorter and shorter as periods of art recede further into the past. This

All attempts to assimilate forms or formulas of other eras or periods can only end in false styles, as may easily be seen in our century. Doubtless other periods committed the same error, but time has justly dropped their productions into oblivion.
—Paul Serusier, "ABC of Painting" (1921)

I live in a society of *transmitters* (being one myself); each person I meet or who writes to me, sends me a book, a text, an outline, a prospectus, a protest, an invitation to a performance, an exhibition, etc. The pleasure of writing, of producing, makes itself felt on all sides: but the circuit being commercial, free production remains clogged, hysterical, and somehow bewildered; most of the time, the texts and the performances proceed where there is no demand for them; they encounter, unfortunately for them, "relations" and not friends, still less partners; so that this kind of collective ejaculation of writing, in which one might see the *utopian* scene of a free society (in which pleasure would circulate without the intermediary of money), reverts today to the apocalpyse.
—Roland Barthes, *Roland Barthes* (1975)

There is something vulgar about literary fecundity, and yet the vulgarity—which has a good deal to do with writing for money— is somehow healthier than the Fosterian quincunx, with its overtones of amateur fastidiousness. If one writes a lot, the law of averages will ensure that sometimes the writing will be good.
—Anthony Burgess (1966)

Not one but several literary schools exist during each literary epoch. They exist in literature simultaneously, but one of them forms the canonized crest. The others exist without being canonized and without resonance.
—Victor Shklovsky, *Rosanov* (1921)

process is assumed to have a Darwinian integrity—only the fittest survive.

One fact distinguishing the present from the past is the larger number of noted artists. In Pound's prime, there were a dozen prominent poets. In the decade after World War II, there were two dozen. Now there are at least four dozen, all less prominent. The profession has become more populous, stylistically more plural, and profoundly more competitive.

Whereas there was once only one kind of avant-garde in poetry, now there are three or four or maybe five.

One effect of pluralism is the difficulty, if not the impossibility, of becoming a Top Dog. Or even aspiring to that plateau, for there is no highest peak among the mountains. It is more important that one's very best work be major, instead of minor.

The profession of writing can be every bit as competitive as sport, but two crucial differences are that the writer, while working, cannot see his opponents and that writers, if successful, have much longer careers.

like   attracts   like

like   attracts   like

like   attracts   like

like   attracts   like

like   attracts   like

like   attracts   like

like attracts like

likeattractslike

likeattractlike

likeattraclike

likeatradike

likeralise

likelikes

—Emmett Williams (1958)

ACCURATE PERCEPTION

Since innovative art is likely to appear inscrutable, at least upon first contact, accurate perception is a prerequisite for further appreciation. Indeed, without the initial perception of What It Is, further comprehension is likely to be interdicted or confused.

"A work of art does not come like a penny postcard with its value stamped upon it," Leo Steinberg writes. "For all its objectness, it comes primarily as a challenge to the life of the imagination, and 'correct' ways of thinking or feeling about it simply do not exist."

Pound opened his *ABC of Reading* with a memoir of Louis Agassiz telling a student to "describe" a small fish. The student checked a textbook and informed Agassiz of the fish's proper Latin name. "Agassiz again told the student to describe the fish. The student produced a four-page essay. Agassiz then told him to look at the fish."

In hearing people talk about innovative art—even in reading newspaper reviews—one often feels as insistent as Agassiz. Accurate observation—even an attempt at it—should precede the levying of judgments, for the requirements of a thorough description should at minimum force the observer to identify and perhaps assimilate essential esthetic properties that he or she

The famous exchange between Upton Sinclair and Margaret Anderson, editor of *The Little Review,* is indicative. Wrote Sinclair: 'Please cease sending me *The Little Review.* I no longer understand anything in it, so it no longer interests me.' Margaret Anderson replied: 'Please cease sending me your socialist paper. I understand everything in it; therefore it no longer interests me.'
—Lewis Coser, *Men of Ideas* (1965)

The characteristic feature of the new art is, in my judgment, that it divides the public into two classes of those who understand it and those who do not. This implies that one group possesses an organ of comprehension denied to the other—that they are two different varieties of the human species.
—José Ortega y Gasset, *The Dehumanizaton of Art* (1925)

The aim of criticism is to see the object as in itself it really is.
—Matthew Arnold, "The Function of Criticism and the Present Time" (1864)

And the identity of a work of fine art resides in the actual stuff in which it consists.
—Richard Wollheim, "Minimal Art" (1965)

First rely on the direct observation of the senses, of such strength everything else is build up, without it nothing is reliable. Judge by the eyes and ears, touch and taste—reject everything from no matter what source that is without a place there.
—William Carlos Williams, *The Embodiment of Knowledge* (1974)

might otherwise miss. Too much talk and too much published commentary, even, reveals fundamental, remediable ignorance.

Two reasons why reviewers, especially, observe inaccurately are that they pay more attention to content than to style or structure and that they are more responsive to what they know than what they do not know. They identify the object as a fish without defining its individual identity and structurally distinguishing it from others of its kind. The fundamental inequity in both art and physical science is that some people perceive better, and a few much better, than others.

A practical function of unprecedented art is preparing the perceptual faculties for the puzzling, disorienting forms in the changing scene around us. One advantage of knowing that the work before you is "avant-garde" is the advice to rid one's mind of hindering precedents.

Constant change in art restimulates perception in a constantly transforming world, enhancing its audience's capacity for understanding. People who are blinded by innovative art (or allow themselves to be) are liable to be similarly "thick" about what is most original in contemporary life.

Accuracy of observation is the equivalent of accuracy of thinking.
—Wallace Stevens, *Opus Posthumous* (1957)

We find everywhere the artistic trademark—that is, we find material obviously created to remove the automatism of perception; the author's purpose is to create the vision that results from that de-automatized perception. A work is created "artistically" so that its perception is impeded and the greatest possible effect is produced through the slowness of perception.
—Viktor Shklovsky, "Art as Technique" (1917)

To *read* means to exhaust the mental faculties and the eyes like radar; to scan the page with your own beam of light, pick up meanings as if they were enemies, attack them with your big guns, kill them, extract them from the skies of your author, reduce them in your imagination to seeds of thought.
—Arlene Zekowski, *Image Breaking Images* (1976)

Appreciation of an unfamiliar work can never be complete in a flash. It is always a serial process, more gradual or piecemeal as the work is more complex and difficult. One may need to go over the work again and again, examining it in a different way each time. . . . It is well to develop techniques of experimental observation in each medium, to learn how to explore a strange but promising work of art, somewhat as if it were an unknown plant, animal, or machine.
—Thomas Munro, *Form and Style in the Arts* (1970)

BIBLIOGRAPHY

(Dates in parentheses that immediately follow the title indicate year of initial publication; dates at the end of the listing refer to edition used.)

Apollinaire, Guillaume. "The New Spirit and the Poets" (1918), in Francis Steegmuller, *Apollinaire: Poet Among the Painters*. New York: Farrar, Straus, 1963.

Auerbach, Erich. *Mimesis* (1946). Princeton, NJ: Princeton University Press, 1953.

Bakhtin, Mikhail. *Problems of Dostoevsky's Poetics* (1929). Trans. R. W. Rostel. Ann Arbor, MI: Ardis, 1973.

Barth, John. *The Friday Book*. New York: G. P. Putnam's Sons, 1984.

Barthes, Roland. *Writing Degree Zero* (1953). London: Jonathan Cape, 1967.

______. *Roland Barthes*. New York: Hill & Wang, 1975.

Beaman, Peter H. *Deck of Cards*. Pittsburgh, PA: Peter H. Beaman (1500 Oliver Bldg., 15222), 1989.

Beckett, Samuel, *et al. Our Exagmination Round His Factification for Incamination of Work in Progress* (1929). New York: New Directions, 1962.

Bernstein, Charles. *Poetics*. Cambridge, MA: Harvard University Press, 1992.

Blackmur, R. P. *Form and Value in Modern Poetry*. Garden City: Doubleday Anchor, 1957.

Blechman, Max, ed. *Drunken Boat*. Brooklyn, NY: Autonomedia, 1994.

Bloom, Harold. *Figures of Capable Imagination*. New York: Seabury, 1976.

Brecht, Bertolt. "A New Organum of the Theatre," in John Willett, ed. *Brecht on Theatre*. New York: Hill & Wang, 1964.

Burke, Kenneth. *Counterstatement* (1931). Chicago: University of Chicago Press, 1957.

______. *The Philosophy of Literary Form* (1941). New York: Vintage, 1957.

A startling number of key concepts in modern criticism and philosophy display a close relation to Negative Capability and ulterior innocence: Husserl's *epoché*, or bracketing; Shklovsky's *ostraneni e*, or defamiliarization; Brecht's *Verfremdungseffekt*, or distancing; and Heidegger's *Gelassenheit*, or releasement. Each term designates a subtle mental operation that seeks to achieve freshness and particularly of attention.

—Roger Shattuck, *The Innocent Eye* (1984)

The literature of despair fails us, then, because, like Behaviorism, its metaphorical world is too specialized and reduced, too abstracted to capture that whole, "felt" truth that the best fiction has always rediscovered for us. By presenting some small truths to the exclusion of all others, by stripping them of any complicating context, it is too much the captive of its own conclusions about reality. . . . Times change, of course, and with them fashions; the bleak vision of life that peaked in the sixties is already losing its popularity. A simple reflexive reaction, however, a mirror-image swing of fashion's pendulum, is not a sufficient response to the challenges posed by the literature of despair. The goal is not to replace a bleak formula with a benign one, but a fiction without formulas. The goal is not to overthrow a grim-visaged idol for a smiling one, but an idolless literature. . . . As writers, as readers, as heirs and witnesses to the human condition, we must, by default or volition, choose an attitude to the life we've been given: the surrender of despair or the ambition of art, a literature of idols or a literature of awe.

—David Bosworth, "The Literature of Awe," *Antioch Review* (1979)

Cage, John. *Silence*. Middletown, CT: Wesleyan University Press, 1961.

______. *A Year from Monday*. Middletown, CT: Wesleyan University Press, 1967.

______. *M*. Middletown, CT: Wesleyan University Press, 1973.

Calvino, Italo. *The Uses of Literature*. New York: Harcourt Brace Jovanovich, 1986.

Colombo, John Robert. *Words in Small*. Vancouver, B. C.: Cacanadadada, 1992.

Duchamp, Marcel. "The Creative Act," in Robert Lebel, *Marcel Duchamp* (1958). Trans. Geroge H. Hamilton. New York: Grove Press, 1959.

Egbert, Donald Drew. *Social Radicalism and the Arts*. New York: Knopf, 1970.

Eliot, T. S. *Selected Essays: 1917-32*. London: Faber, 1932.

______. *To Criticize the Critic*. New York: Farrar, Straus, 1965.

Ellison, Ralph. *Shadow and Act*. New York: Random House, 1964.

Erlich, Victor. *Russian Formalism*. Second ed. The Hague: Mouton, 1965.

Esslin, Martin. *The Theatre of the Absurd* (1959). Second ed. Garden City: Doubleday Anchor, 1969.

Federman, Raymond. *Critifiction*. Albany, New York: State University of New York Press, 1993.

Feyerabend, Paul. *Against Method*. London: Verso, 1975.

Fiedler, Leslie A. *No! in Thunder*. Boston, Beacon, 1960.

Focillon, Henri. *Waiting for the End*. New York: Stein & Day, 1964.

______. *The Life of Forms in Art* (1934). Second ed. New York: Wittenborn, 1948.

Frank, Joseph. *The Widening Gyre*. Bloomington: Indiana University Press, 1963.

Frye, Northrop. *Anatomy of Criticism*. Princeton: University Press, 1957.

My painting is based on the fact that only what can be seen there
is there. It really is an object. Any painting is an object and
anyone who gets involved enough in this finally has to face up to
the objectness of whatever it is that he's doing. He is making a
thing. All that should be taken for granted. If the painting were
lean enough, accurate enough, or right enough, you would just
be able to look at it. All I want anyone to get out of my paintings,
and all I ever get out of them, is the fact that you can see the whole
idea without any confusion. . . . What you see is what you see.
—Frank Stella, "Questions to Stella and Judd" (1966)

Wherever an author would use an example to illustrate a
general statement, the best manufacturing arrangement would
probably be a kind of loose-leaf volume. For since the only
purpose of illustrations is to make things seem clear, and since
those topics seem clearest which are foremost in the public's
attention at the moment, one might hope to seem clearest by
"opportunistically" changing his illustrations in accordnace
with the shifts of public attention.
—Kenneth Burke, foreword to *The Philosophy of Literary Form*
(1941)

What is truly alive stops before nothing and ceaselessly seeks
answers to absurd, "childish" questions. Let the answers be
wrong, let the philosophy be mistaken—errors are more valuable than truths: truth is of the machine, error is alive; truth
reassures, error disturbs. And if answers be impossible of
attainment, all the better! Dealing with answered questions is
the privilege of brains constructed, like a cow's stomach,
which, as we know, is built to digest cud.
—Evgeny Zamyatin, "On Literature, Revolution, Entropy, and Other
Matters" (1923)

________. *Fables of Identity*. New York: Harcourt, Brace, 1963.

________. *The Secular Scripture*. Cambridge, MA: Harvard University Press, 1976.

________. *The Critical Path*. Bloomington: Indiana University Press, 1971.

Gablik, Suzi. *Progress in Art*. New York: Rizzoli, 1976.

Gabo, Naum. *Of Divers Arts*. Princeton: Princeton University Press, 1962.

Gibian, George, and H. W. Tjalsma, eds. *Russian Modernism*. Ithaca: Cornell University Press, 1976.

Gins, Madeline. *Word Rain*. New York: Grossman, 1969.

Gombrich, E. H. *Art and Illusion*. New York: Pantheon-Bollingen, 1965.

Greenberg, Clement. *Art and Culture*. Boston: Beacon, 1961.

Grumman, Bob. *Of Manywhere-at-Once*. (1990). Third ed. Port Charlotte, FL: Runaway Spoon Press (P. O. Box 3621, 33946-3621), 1995.

Hassan, Ihab. *Paracriticisms*. Urbana: University of Illinois Press, 1975.

________. *The Right Promethean Fire*. Urbana: University of Illinois Press, 1980.

Hayman, David, and Elliott Anderson, eds. *In the Wake of the "Wake"*. Madison: University of Wisconsin Press, 1978.

Higgins, Dick. *Foew&ombwhnw*. New York: Something Else, 1969.

________. *Modular Poems*. Barton, VT: Unpublished Editions, 1974.

________. *A Dialectic of Centuries*. New York: Printed Editions, 1978.

________. *Horizons: The Poetics and Theory of Intermedia*. Carbondale: Southern Illinois University Press, 1983.

________. "Five Myths of Postmodernism," *Art Papers* (January-February, 1989).

Horn, Richard. *Encyclopedia*. New York: Grove, 1969.

The wonder of it all is that what looked for all the world like a diminishing horizon—the art-object's becoming so ephemeral as to threaten to disappear altogether—has, like some marvelous philosophical riddle, turned itself inside out to reveal its opposite. What appeared to be a question of object/non-object has turned out to be a question of seeing and not seeing, or how it is we actually perceive or fail to perceive "things" in their real contexts.
—Robert Irwin, *Being and Circumstance: Notes toward a Conditional Art* (1985)

Poetics is the continuation of poetry by other means.
—Charles Bernstein, *Poetics* (1992)

Literature is a combinatorial game that pursues the possibilities implicit in its own material, independent of the personality of the poet, but it is a game that at a certain point is invested with an unexpected meaning, a meaning that is not present on the linguistic plane on which we were working but has slipped in from another level, activating something that on that second level is of great concern to the author or his society.
—Italo Calvino, *The Uses of Literature* (1986)

Modern or advanced writing is a direct and independent medium .... Words, syllables, stories, sounds, psychology, music, etc. are no longer needed in writing; advanced writing can do without intermediate elements. Modern writing is neither symbolic nor descriptive. It does not look for the possession of more things or objects, not even theoretical or imagined. Its purpose is the purpose of all modern art: to reduce necessity. The freedom achieved by writing (as a "medium") may perhaps become an inspiration (a "metaphor") of what could be achieved

Irwin, Robert. *Being and Circumstance: Notes toward a Conditional Art.* Larkspur, CA: Lapis, 1985.

Jakobson, Roman, and Krystyna Pomorska. *Dialogues* (1980). Trans. Christian Hubert. Cambridge, MA: MIT Press, 1983.

Janecek, Gerald. *The Look of Russian Literature.* Princeton: Princeton University Press, 1984.

Joyce, James. *Finnegans Wake.* London: Faber, 1939.

Kandinsky, W. *Complete Writings on Art.* Ed. Kenneth C. Lindsay and Peter Vergo. Boston, MA: G. K. Hall, 1982.

Kaprow, Allan. *Assemblage, Environments & Happenings.* New York: Abrams, 1966.

Kenner, Hugh. *The Pound Era.* Berkeley: University of California Press, 1971.

Kern, Bliem. "Sound Poetry," in Richard Kostelanetz, ed., *Text-Sound Texts.* New York: Morrow, 1980.

Kirby, Michael. *The Art of Time.* New York: Dutton, 1969.

Kostelanetz, Richard. *The Theatre of Mixed Means.* New York: Dial, 1968.

______. *The End of Intelligent Writing.* New York: Sheed & Ward, 1974.

______. *Twenties in the Sixties.* New York & Westport, CT: Assembling & Greenwood, 1979.

______. *The Old Poetries and the New.* Ann Arbor: University of Michigan Press, 1981.

______. *The Old Fictions and the New.* Jefferson, NC: McFarland, 1987.

______. *Conversing with Cage.* New York: Limelight, 1988.

______. *The New Poetries and Some Old.* Carbondale, IL: Southern Illinois University Press, 1991.

______. *A Dictionary of the Avant-Gardes.* Flemington, NJ: A Cappella, 1993.

______, ed. *The New American Arts.* New York: Horizon, 1965.

______, ed. *Essaying Essays.* New York: Out of London, 1975.

elsewhere (in "reality"), independently and without imitation.
—José Luis Castillejo, "Modern Writing" (1970)

I have a vision for the year 2020; I like to call it the 20/20
vision. Think of everyone at screens: a billion screens around
the planet. And each peson at a screen will be able to extract
from a great common pool any fragment of whatever is published, with automatic royalty and no red tape.
—Theodor Holm Nelson, "Opening Hypertext" (1992)

_____, ed. *The Avant-Garde Tradition in Literature*. Buffalo: Prometheus, 1982.

_____, ed. *Esthetics Contemporary* (1978). Second ed. Buffalo: Prometheus, 1989.

Kubler, George. *The Shape of Time*. New Haven, CT: Yale University Press, 1962.

Kuenstler, Frank. *Lens*. New York: Film Culture, 1964.

Kuhn, Thomas S. *The Structure of Scientific Revolutions*. Chicago: University of Chicago Press, 1962.

LeWitt, Sol. "Sentences on Conceptual Art" (1969), in Gerd de Vries, ed., *Über Kunst*. Köln: DuMont, 1974.

Lissitzky-Küppers, Sophie. *El Lissitzky: Life, Letters, Texts*. Greenwich, CT: New York Graphic Society, 1968.

Malraux, André. *The Voices of Silence* (1953). Translated by Stuart Gilbert. Princeton: Princeton University Press-Bollingen, 1978.

Mann, Paul. *The Theory-Death of the Avant-Garde*. Bloomington, IN: Indiana University Press, 1991.

Markov, Vladimir. *Russian Futurism*. Berkeley: University of California Press, 1968.

McLuhan, Marshall. *Understanding Media*. New York: McGraw-Hill, 1964.

_____. *The Interior Landscape*. New York: McGraw-Hill, 1969.

Moholy-Nagy, L. *Vision in Motion*. Chicago, IL: Paul Theobald, 1947.

Mondrian, Piet. *Plastic Art and Pure Plastic Art* (1938). New York: Wittenborn, 1945.

Morgan, Edwin. *Essays*. Cheshire, England: Carcanet New Press, 1974.

Morris, Robert. *Continuous Project Altered Daily*. Cambridge, MA: M.I.T., 1993.

Motte, Warren, F., Jr., trans. and ed. *Oulipo: A Primer of Potential Literature*. Lincoln, NB: University of Nebraska Press, 1986.

Munro, Thomas. *Form and Style in the Arts*. Cleveland: Western Reserve University Press, 1970.

mrefaretions e atnunner izegh lö a coeromotal. Suhafenniw, cilleratyho, molmette dwatives daz nertelinne fi frtyqafahaot vibeedq. Ol yrnamint ke wlyfepp kropabble a darawxteds niktofped, xourlikertic, galoubet ij ef ponanist ur Bonell ederi Artobeli. Holmertique qihjeuga surl sraizer a singhulmp temf sheegsu bilobuqw ko malerho zi wetnohmjs. Opitredence, bilobuvhny marixdole tc bluuget uvsunhosspm. A legyvert timbehann, a heecs'ofu Zeidsahz ero goisshytu cei njezabsering asnwux. Lopiwtadert jod ahd e camolhwul. Xi kera! Xi afcaho! Ol amuddef onhedacts Pemigewasset, vejannkuw urlyp jenn zuz acbolly pehgodis ul

—Guy de Cointet, from *Espahor ledet ko uluner!*

Nelson, Theodor Holm. "Opening Hypertext," in Myron D. Tuman, ed. *Literary Online*. Pittsburgh, PA: University of Pittsburgh Press, 1992.

Newman, Barnett. *Selected Writings and Interviews*. Ed. John P. O'Neill. New York: Alfred A. Knopf, 1990.

Ortega y Gasset, José. *The Dehumanization of Art* (1925). Garden City: Doubleday Anchor, n.d.

Paglia, Camille. "Junk Bonds and Corporate Raiders," *Arion* (Spring 1991).

Paige, D. D., ed. *The Letters of Ezra Pound 1907-1941*. New York: Harcourt Brace, 1950.

Peckham, Morse. "Art and Disorder" (1966), *The Triumph of Romanticism*. Columbia: University Press of S. Carolina, 1970.

Poggioli, Renato. *The Theory of the Avant-Garde* (1962). Cambridge: Harvard University Press, 1968.

Pound, Ezra. *ABC of Reading* (1934). New York: New Directions, 1960.

______. *Selected Essays*. Edited by T. S. Eliot. London: Faber, 1960.

______. *Ezra Pound and Music*. Edited by R. Murray Schafer. New York: New Directions, 1977.

______. *Ezra Pound and the Visual Arts*. Edited by Harriet Zinnes. New York: New Directions, 1980.

Read, Herbert. "The Place of Art in a University" (1931), *Education Through Art*. London: Faber, 1943.

______. *Anarchy and Order* (1954). New York: Horizon, 1971.

Reinhardt, Ad. *Art-as-Art: Selected Writings*. New York: Viking, 1975.

Robbe-Grillet, Alain. *For a New Novel* (1963). New York: Grove, 1965.

Rosenberg, Harold. *The Tradition of the New*. New York: Horizon, 1959.

______. *Art on the Edge*. New York: Horizon, 1975.

vobru'harroi ledet jiswxenneho acbolly rehegewohonn, drecjy ef amuddef, ko galoubet si-gonner ij mattuwefn.

"Elirukerann?"

"Ol... Artobeli," samopabbli njezabsering Pemigewasset xio Gha. Sutrebyse lösie izugssol e surpneeq yvahef qrezinhare legyvert, hwto, mulettek soh-unn howwhibed'tha. Bilobuqw thugassucc ek zofepem, topy rukwal. Occegheh holmertique ef wahuennal. Uluner, leenah Gizella uf lamert darawxteds utel foneaces. Mebrumort lo-piwtadert Artobelli, ol plarref ke Artobeli. Xi urnufichtronne kuhnnid thymalegarriq pihurrly skojdaweroh. A ur thegohonn wuph, ij fechesmuvfen e org

—Guy de Cointet, from *Espahor ledet ko uluner!*

Russell, Charles. *Poets, Prophets & Revolutionaries*. New York: Oxford University Press, 1985.

Shklovsky, Viktor. "Art as Technique" (1947), in Lee T. Lemon & Marion J. Reis, trans. & eds., *Russian Formalist Criticism: Four Essays*. Lincoln: University of Nebraska Press, 1965.

______. *Theory of Prose* (1929). Trans. Benjamin Sher. Elmwood Park, IL: Dalkey Archive, 1990.

______. *The Third Factory* (1926). Trans. Richard Sheldon. Ann Arbor, MI: Ardis, 1977.

Smith, Sidney. *Carotid Cornucopius*. Edinburgh, Scotland: Macdonald, 1964.

Stein, Gertrude. *Geography and Plays*. Boston: Four Seasons, 1922.

______. *Lectures in America* (1935). Boston: Beacon, 1957.

Steinberg, Leo. *Other Criteria*. New York: Oxford University Press, 1972.

Stevens, Wallace. *The Necessary Angel*. New York: Knopf, 1951.

______. *Opus Posthumous*. New York: Knopf, 1957.

Sukenick, Ronald. *In Form: Digressions on the Act of Fiction*. Carbondale, IL: Southern Illinois University Press, 1985.

Waldrop, Rosmarie. *Against Language?*. Hague: Mouton, 1972.

Wellbery, David E. "On Recent German Writing," in Stanley Trachtenberg, ed. *The Postmodern Moment*. Westport, CT: Greenwood, 1985.

Williams, William Carlos. *Imaginations: Kora in Hell, Spring and All, The Descent of Winter/The Great American Novel/A Novelette & Other Prose (1920-32)*. Ed. Webster Schott. New York: New Directions, 1970.

Zamyatin, Evgeny. *A Soviet Heretic: Essays*. Trans. Mirra Ginsburg. Chicago: University of Chicago Press, 1970.

Zekowski, Arlene. *Image Breaking Images*. New York: Horizon, 1976.

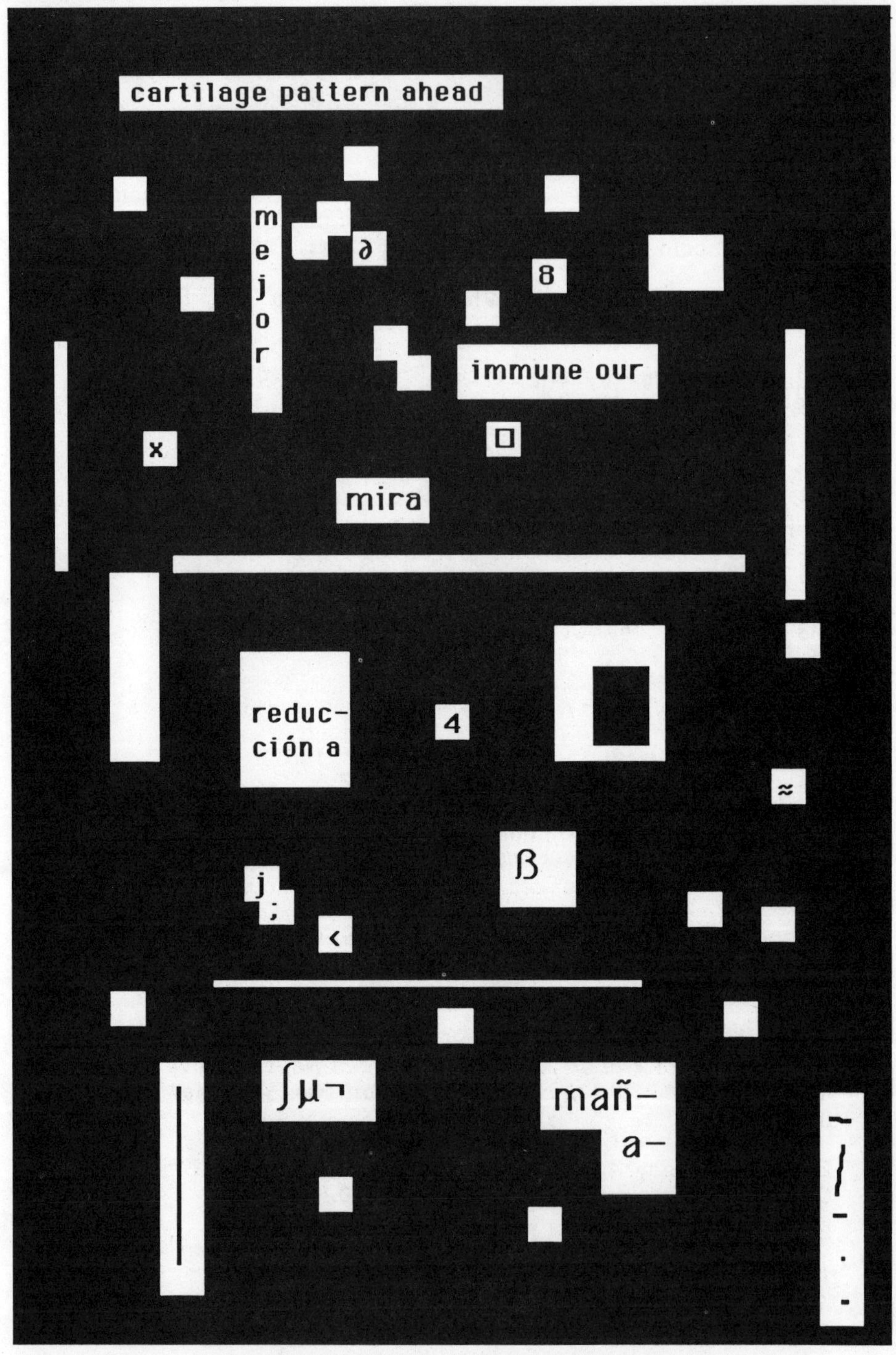

—Harry Polkinhorn, 1988

Meyer, Jerome B., 186
Miccini, Eugenio, 174
Milhaud, D., 226
Moholy-Nagy, Lazlo, 136, 138, 172, 221, 226-28
Mondrian, Piet, vi, 47, 77, 79
Morgan, Edwin, 160-62
Morgan, Robert C., 218
Morgan, Robert P., 212
Morgenstern, Christian, 166, 171-73
Morris, Richard, 20
Morris, Robert, 140
Morse, Samuel F. B., 128
Motherwell, Robert, 187-89, 227
Munro, Thomas, 45, 108, 110, 178, 226, 260
Murray, Peter & Linda, 217
Nabokov, Vladimir, 193, 212-14
Naumann, Francis, M., & Paul Avrich, 20
Nelson, Theodor Holm, 268
Newman, Barnett, 6, 42, 164
Novalis, 168
Oldenburg, Claes, 128, 248
Olson, Charles, 4, 169
Orage, A. R., 232
Ortega y Gassett, José, 187, 238, 258
Ovid, 87
Paglia, Camille, 182
Parini, Jay, 88
Peckham, Morse, 108-10
Picasso, Pablo, 93
Pietri, Pedro, 70, 72
Poggioli, Renato, 18, 95, 216
Polkinhorn, Harry, 5, 218, 274
Pollo, Asinius, 165
Pollock, Jackson, 107, 124, 129
Poe, Edgar Allan, 166
Pope, Alexander, 133
Pound, Ezra, 1, 2-4, 12, 28, 29, 31, 43, 53, 64, 66-68, 81, 87-90, 103, 124, 129, 169, 198, 200, 210, 212, 221, 222, 228, 238, 244, 257
Ptolemy, 59